Holt McDougal
Algebra 1

Larson   Boswell   Kanold   Stiff

Using the Algebra 1 Remediation Book

The Algebra 1 Remediation Book is separated into five major subdivisions that help mark progress through the course. Each major subdivision is broken into 5 to 6 major topics. Each major topic contains 3 to 7 half page lessons, and a quiz that assesses the student's understanding. The lessons provide examples, vocabulary, helpful hints, and exercises.

HOLT McDOUGAL

HOUGHTON MIFFLIN HARCOURT

Printed in the U.S.A.

ISBN 978-0-54771069-3

2 3 4 5 7 8 9 10   1421   20 19 18 17 16 15 14 13 12

4500349551   ^ B C D E F G

Contents

BENCHMARK 1
(Chapters 1 and 2)

A. Expressions, Equations, and Inequalities

A **variable** is a letter used to represent one or more numbers. An **algebraic expression** is made from numbers, variables, and algebraic operations. The following examples describe how expressions can be evaluated, combined, written, and used to write algebraic equations and inequalities.

1. Evaluate Expressions

Vocabulary

Evaluate an expression Substitute a number for the variable, perform the operation(s), and simplify the result if necessary.

EXAMPLE

When a number is followed directly by a variable, the operation of multiplication is always implied.

Evaluate the expression.

a. $16n$ when $n = 4$ **b.** $\frac{25}{k}$ when $k = 5$ **c.** $h - 8$ when $h = 12.2$

d. $\frac{4}{3} + h$ when $h = \frac{1}{3}$ **e.** x^3 when $x = 4$ **f.** a^2 when $a = 1.2$

Solution:

a. $16n = 16 \cdot 4$ **b.** $\frac{25}{k} = \frac{25}{5}$ **c.** $h - 8 = 12.2 - 8$

$= 64$ $= 5$ $= 4.2$

d. $\frac{4}{3} + h = \frac{4}{3} + \frac{1}{3}$ **e.** $x^3 = 4^3$ **f.** $a^2 = 1.2^2$

$= \frac{5}{3}$ $= 4 \cdot 4 \cdot 4$ $= (1.2)(1.2)$

                       $= 64$ $= 1.44$

PRACTICE

Evaluate the expression.

1. $5b$ when $b = 6$ **2.** $\frac{42}{h}$ when $h = 14$

3. $14 - b$ when $b = 11.3$ **4.** $v + \frac{7}{6}$ when $v = \frac{1}{3}$

5. y^4 when $y = 3$ **6.** q^2 when $q = 2.1$

2. Order of Operations

Vocabulary

Order of operations Established rule for evaluating an expression involving more than one operation:

     Step 1: Evaluate expressions inside grouping symbols.

     Step 2: Evaluate powers.

     Step 3: Multiply and **divide** from left to right.

     Step 4: Add and **subtract** from left to right.

BENCHMARK 1
(Chapters 1 and 2)

EXAMPLE   **Evaluate the expression.**

a. $3 \cdot 2^4 - 5 \cdot 6$ **b.** $4(3^2 + 5)$ **c.** $5[12 - (4 + 5)]$

Solution:

The multiplication that could be written in two steps $(3 \cdot 16$ evaluated first, followed by $5 \cdot 6)$ is combined as one step.

a. $3 \cdot 2^4 - 5 \cdot 6 = 3 \cdot 16 - 5 \cdot 6$ **Evaluate power.**
$$= 48 - 30$$ **Multiply.**
$$= 18$$ **Subtract.**

b. $4(3^2 + 5) = 4(9 + 5)$ **Evaluate power.**
$$= 4(14)$$ **Add within parentheses.**
$$= 56$$ **Multiply.**

c. $5[12 - (4 + 5)] = 5(12 - 9)$ **Add within parentheses.**
$$= 5(3)$$ **Subtract within brackets.**
$$= 15$$ **Multiply.**

PRACTICE   **Evaluate the expression.**

7. $4(10 - 3) - 5 \cdot 2$ **8.** $21 + (3^2 - 4)$ **9.** $2[42 \div (9 - 3)]$

3. Write Expressions

EXAMPLE   **Translate verbal phrases into expressions.**

Keep a glossary of terms that describe each of the four basic operations.

a. The product of 8 and m increased by 5

b. The quotient of 8 and the difference of a number x and 2

c. The sum of 20 and the square of a number n

Solution:

a. $8m + 5$ **b.** $\dfrac{8}{x - 2}$ **c.** $20 + n^2$

PRACTICE   **Translate the verbal phrases into expressions.**

10. The quotient when the quantity of a number y increased by 4 is divided by 6

11. 4 less than twice the square of a number q

12. 8 more than the product of a number w and 6

4. Write Equations and Inequalities

Vocabulary

Open sentence A mathematical statement that contains two expressions and a symbol that compares them.

Equation An open sentence that contains the symbol $=$.

Inequality An open sentence that contains one of the symbols $<$, $\leq$, $>$, or $\geq$.

BENCHMARK 1
(Chapters 1 and 2)

EXAMPLE

"No less than" ($\geq$) and "no greater than" ($\leq$) are opposites of "less than" ($<$) and "greater than" ($>$), respectively.

Write an equation or an inequality.

a. The difference of a number p and 12 is at most 15.

b. The product of 5 and a number m is 14.

c. A number x is at least 6 and less than 9.

Solution:

a. $p - 12 \leq 15$ **b.** $5m = 14$ **c.** $6 \leq x < 9$

PRACTICE

Write an equation or inequality.

13. The quotient of 12 and a number q is at most 5.

14. The sum of twice a number h and 5 is the same as 23.

15. The difference of a number w and 4 is greater than 12 and no more than 20.

Quiz

Evaluate the expression.

1. $\dfrac{h}{3} + \dfrac{1}{3}$ when $h = 5$ **2.** $\dfrac{64}{b^2}$ when $b = 4$ **3.** $12 - \dfrac{5a}{4}$ when $a = 4$

Evaluate the expression.

4. $(4^2 - 3) \cdot (2 + 3) + 1$ **5.** $4[(2^2 - 3) + 1]$ **6.** $\dfrac{[54 \div (6 - 3)^2]^2}{8 - 2}$

Translate the verbal phrases into expressions.

7. The product of twice the number y and 4 increased by 8

8. The difference of 6 times the square of a number x and 15

Write an equation or inequality.

9. The sum of the number b and 12 is twice the number b.

10. The product of a number q and 3 is no less than 10 and no more than 15.

BENCHMARK 1
(Chapters 1 and 2)

B. Problem Solving

One way to try solving a math problem is to use an organized strategy, or problem-solving plan. Read the problem to find what information is given and what you need to find out. Decide on the strategy you will use, and apply it to solve the problem. Finally, check that your solution makes sense.

1. Check Possible Solutions

Vocabulary

Solution of an equation or inequality A number that can be substituted for the variable in an equation or inequality to make a true statement.

EXAMPLE **Check whether the given number is a solution of the equation or inequality.**

a. $2x - 8 = -2; 3$ **b.** $\frac{x}{3} + 1 = 7; 6$ **c.** $x - 5 \le 3; 2$

Solution:

a. $2(3) - 8 \overset{?}{=} -2$ **b.** $\frac{6}{3} + 1 \overset{?}{=} 7$ **c.** $2 - 5 \overset{?}{\le} 3$

$6 - 8 \overset{?}{=} -2$ $2 + 1 \overset{?}{=} 7$ $-3 \le 3$ ✔

$-2 = -2$ ✔ $3 \neq 7$ ✘

3 is a solution.   6 is *not* a solution.   2 is a solution.

PRACTICE **Check whether the given number is a solution of the equation or inequality.**

1. $5 + a < 10; -4$ **2.** $\frac{n-3}{12} = 1; 4$ **3.** $\frac{r}{4} + 3 = 5; -2$

4. $-8p - 6 \le 0; -1$ **5.** $9d - 3 = 60; 7$ **6.** $m + 8 > -7; -14$

2. Read and Understand a Problem

EXAMPLE **Read the problem below. Identify what you know and what you need to find out. You do not need to solve the problem.**

There may be more than one method that can be used to solve a problem.

You run in a city where the short blocks on north-south streets are 0.03 miles long. The long blocks on east-west streets are 0.2 mile long. You will run 2 long blocks east, a number of short blocks south, 2 long blocks west, then back to your starting point. You want to run 1.1 miles. How many short blocks should you run?

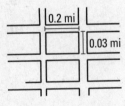

Solution:

What do you know? Each short block is 0.03 miles long. Each long block is 0.2 miles long. You will run 4 long blocks total (2 east + 2 west). You will run *s* short blocks total (south and north). You want to run a total of 2 miles.

What do you want to find out? How many short blocks should you run so that the distance you run on short blocks and the distance you run on 4 long blocks makes a total of 1.1 miles?

BENCHMARK 1
(Chapters 1 and 2)

PRACTICE

7. Read the problem below. Identify what you know and what you need to find out. You do not need to solve the problem.

A bicycle park has a long trail and a short trail. The long trail is 5 km long. The short trail is 2 km long. You will ride 3 laps on the short trail and some number of laps on the long trail. You want to ride 21 km. How many laps should you ride on the long trail?

start/finish

2 km

5 km

3. Make a Plan

EXAMPLE   **Write a verbal model of the statement below.**

How many short blocks should you run so that the distance you run on short blocks and the distance you run on 4 long blocks makes a total of 1.1 miles?

Solution:

$$\underset{\text{(miles)}}{\begin{array}{c}\textbf{Distance run on}\\\textbf{short blocks}\end{array}} + \underset{\text{(miles)}}{\begin{array}{c}\textbf{Distance run on}\\\textbf{long blocks}\end{array}} = \underset{\text{(miles)}}{\begin{array}{c}\textbf{Total}\\\textbf{distance}\end{array}}$$

$$\underset{\text{(miles/block)}}{\begin{array}{c}\textbf{Length of a}\\\textbf{short block}\end{array}} \cdot \underset{\text{(block)}}{\begin{array}{c}\textbf{Number of}\\\textbf{short blocks}\end{array}} + \underset{\text{(miles/block)}}{\begin{array}{c}\textbf{Length of a}\\\textbf{long block}\end{array}} \cdot \underset{\text{(block)}}{\begin{array}{c}\textbf{Number of}\\\textbf{long blocks}\end{array}} = \underset{\text{(miles)}}{\begin{array}{c}\textbf{Total}\\\textbf{distance}\end{array}}$$

PRACTICE

8. Write a verbal model for the problem in Exercise 7.

4. Use Precision and Measurement

Vocabulary   **Precision** is the level of detail that an instrument can measure.

Significant digits are the digits in a measurement that carry meaning contributing to the precision of the measurement.

EXAMPLE   **Determine the number of significant digits in each measurement.**

   a. 7.605 km   **b.** 340 mL   **c.** 0.270 g

Solution

   a. The digits 7, 6, and 5 are nonzero digits, so they are significant digits. The zero is between significant digits, so it is also a significant digit.

      There are 4 significant digits: 7.605.

   b. The digits 3 and 4 are nonzero digits, so they are significant digits. The zero at the end of the whole number is not significant.

      There are 2 significant digits: 340.

   c. The digits 2 and 7 are nonzero digits, so they are significant digits. The zero to the right of the last nonzero digit is also to the right of the decimal point, so it is a significant digit.

      There are 3 significant digits: 0.270.

BENCHMARK 1
(Chapters 1 and 2)

PRACTICE   **Determine the number of significant digits in each measurement.**

9. 3.08 cm   **10.** 18.30 sec   **11.** 0.0075 km

12. 42.10 mi   **13.** 5.625 lb   **14.** 2000 y

Quiz

Check whether the given number is a solution of the equation or inequality.

1. $6 + j < 4; -1$

2. $\dfrac{n+5}{2} = 6; 7$

3. $\dfrac{m}{3} - 8 = -5; 9$

4. $-2y + 3 \le 0; 2$

5. $4g - 5 = 35; 10$

6. $b + 12 > 0; -13$

Read the problem below. Identify what you know and what you need to find out. Then, write a verbal model of the problem. You do not need to solve the problem.

7. Jim's grandmother exercises by walking the main rectangular hall of a local shopping mall. She walks 90 yards down the length of the hall, turns right, and walks 20 yards across the width of the hall. Then, she turns right and walks up the length of the hall again. Finally, she turns right one more time, and walks 20 yards across the width of the hall and ends up at her starting point. Jim's grandmother wants to walk 970 yards. She will walk the length of the hall 9 times. How many times will she walk across the width of the hall?

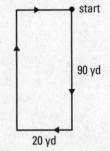

start

90 yd

20 yd

Determine the number of significant digits in each measurement.

8. 20.30 g   **9.** 0.0039 in.   **10.** 100 min

Name _____ Date _____

BENCHMARK 1
(Chapters 1 and 2)

C. Representations of Functions

Functions can be represented by mapping diagrams, tables, verbal or algebraic function rules, and graphs. Each input value and its corresponding output value make up an ordered pair. An ordered pair can be written as (*input, output*) or plotted as a point on a coordinate grid.

1. Identify the Domain and Range of a Function

Vocabulary **Function** A pairing of input values to output values, where the value of each output depends on the value of the corresponding input, and each input corresponds to exactly one output.

Domain The set of input values for a function.

Range The set of output values for a function.

EXAMPLE **Identify the domain and range of the function.**

a.

Input	Output
0	10
1	11
2	12
3	13

b.

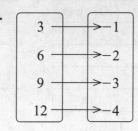

c.

Input	Output
−8	−4
4	2
6	3
10	5

Solution:

a. Domain: 0, 1, 2, 3

   Range: 10, 11, 12, 13

b. Domain: 3, 6, 9, 12

   Range: −1, −2, −3, −4

c. Domain: −8, 4, 6, 10

   Range: −4, 2, 3, 5

PRACTICE **Identify the domain and range of each function.**

1.

Input	Output
0	1
1	3
2	5
3	7

2.

Input	Output
−5	1
−10	2
−15	3
−20	4

3.

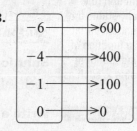

BENCHMARK 1
(Chapters 1 and 2)

EXAMPLE   **Tell whether the pairing is a function.**

a.

Input	Output
−6	2
−7	3
−8	4
−9	5

b.

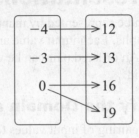

c.

Input	Output
35	0
40	5
40	10
45	15

Solution:

a. Yes

b. No; 0 maps to two outputs.

c. No; 40 maps to two outputs.

PRACTICE   **Tell whether the pairing is a function.**

4.

Input	Output
−14	4
−8	4
−2	4
4	4

5.

Input	Output
9	0
15	6
27	18
35	26

6.

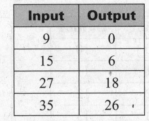

2. Write a Function Rule

Vocabulary   **Independent variable** A function's input variable.

Dependent variable A function's output variable.

EXAMPLE   **Write a rule for the function.**

A function rule usually states the dependent variable y as a function of the independent variable x, such as $y = x + 3$.

Input, x	0	1	2	3	4
Output, y	0	3	6	9	12

Solution:

Each value of y is 3 times the corresponding x value. The function rule is $y = 3x$.

PRACTICE   **Write a rule for the function.**

7.

Input, x	−4	−2	0	2	4
Output, y	−2	−1	0	1	2

8.

Input, x	5	10	15	20	25
Output, y	1	6	11	16	21

9.

Input, x	3	5	9	12	16
Output, y	12	14	18	21	25

10.

Input, x	−6	−2	3	7	8
Output, y	6	2	−3	−7	−8

Name _____   Date _____

BENCHMARK 1
(Chapters 1 and 2)

3. Make a Table for a Function

EXAMPLE   **Make a table for the function and identify the range of the function.**

$y = x + 2.6$

Domain: 2, 3, 4, 5, 6

Solution:

Input, *x*	2	3	4	5	6
Output, *y*	4.6	5.6	6.6	7.6	8.6

Range: 4.6, 5.6, 6.6, 7.6, 8.6

PRACTICE   **Make a table for the function and identify the range of the function.**

11. $y = \dfrac{2}{3}x$ **12.** $y = x - 1.1$ **13.** $y = -2x + 5$

Domain: 3, 6, 9, 12, 15   Domain: $-5, -4, -3, -2, -1$ Domain: 1, 2, 4, 7, 9

14. $y = \dfrac{x + 1}{2}$ **15.** $y = x + 14$ **16.** $y = -5x$

Domain: 20, 30, 40, 50, 60   Domain: 2, 5, 6, 8, 9   Domain: $-3, -1, 4, 8, 11$

4. Graph a Function

EXAMPLE   **Graph the function $y = x - 2$ with domain 4, 5, 6, 7, and 8.**

Solution:

Step 1: Make an input-output table.

Input, *x*	4	5	6	7	8
Output, *y*	2	3	4	5	6

Step 2: List the ordered pairs (x, y).

(4, 2), (5, 3), (6, 4), (7, 5), (8, 6)

Step 3: Plot a point for each ordered pair (x, y).

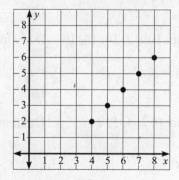

PRACTICE   **Graph the function.**

17. $y = x - 3$ **18.** $y = \dfrac{1}{3}x$ **19.** $y = 3x - 3$

Domain: 5, 7, 10, 13, 15   Domain: 3, 9, 15, 21, 27   Domain: 1, 2, 3, 4, 5

BENCHMARK 1
(Chapters 1 and 2)

20. $y = 1.5x + 2$

Domain: 0, 3, 4, 6, 9

21. $y = \frac{1}{2}x - 2$

Domain: 4, 5, 7, 8, 10

22. $y = \frac{x + 2}{3}$

Domain: 1, 4, 7, 10, 13

Quiz

Identify the domain and range of each function.

1.

Input	Output
7	23
10	35
14	51
17	63

2.

Input	Output
−10	90
−8	54
−5	15
−4	6

3.

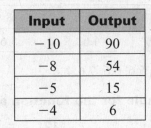

Tell whether each pairing is a function.

4.

Input	Output
5	8
8	5
8	4
10	3

5.

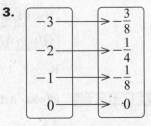

6.

Input	Output
−5	−2
2	5
7	10
11	14

Write a rule for the function.

7.

Input, x	−5	−3	0	4	6
Output, y	−25	−15	0	20	30

8.

Input, x	2	4	5	7	10
Output, y	−4	−8	−10	−14	−20

9.

Input, x	3	6	8	10	13
Output, y	−4	−1	1	3	6

10.

Input, x	10	24	32	48	50
Output, y	15	36	48	72	75

Make a table for the function and identify the range of the function.

11. $y = -4x + 10$

Domain: −3, −1, 2, 5, 6

12. $y = \frac{3}{4}x - 1$

Domain: 10, 12, 14, 16, 18

13. $y = \frac{2x + 3}{4}$

Domain: 1, 9, 13, 19, 23

Graph the function.

14. $y = x - 6$

Domain: 6, 7, 8, 9, 10

15. $y = 5x$

Domain: 0, 2, 4, 5, 9

16. $y = -x + 4$

Domain: 0, 1, 2, 3, 4

BENCHMARK 1
(Chapters 1 and 2)

D. Solving Equations in One Variable

To solve an equation in one variable, isolate the variable on one side of the equation. The following examples illustrate different ways to isolate the variable.

1. Order Real Numbers

To order real numbers from least to greatest, graph them first. Then read the numbers from left to right.

EXAMPLE

Order the numbers from least to greatest: $-\frac{4}{5}$, -4.5, -5, $-\sqrt{4}$.

To order numbers, it is sometimes helpful to write decimal approximations of rational and irrational numbers.

Solution:

In order from least to greatest, the numbers are -5, -4.5, $-\sqrt{4}$, and $-\frac{4}{5}$.

PRACTICE   **Order each group of numbers from least to greatest.**

1. $1.23, 1\frac{2}{3}, \frac{3}{2}, \sqrt{3}$ **2.** $0.08, -1.9, -\sqrt{0.04}, \sqrt{2}$ **3.** $6.01, \sqrt{6}, 6\frac{1}{6}, 6.1$

2. Solve an Equation Using Addition or Subtraction

Vocabulary

Inverse operations Two operations that undo each other, such as addition and subtraction or multiplication and division.

Equivalent equations Equations that have the same solution(s).

EXAMPLE   **Use addition or subtraction to solve the equation.**

a. $x + 9 = 3$ **b.** $x - 5 = 2$ **c.** $x + 4.1 = 6$

Solution:

Be sure to subtract (or add) the same number from each side, so that the new equation is *equivalent* to the original equation.

a. $x + 9 = 3$ Write original equation.
   $x + 9 - 9 = 3 - 9$ Use subtraction property of equality. Subtract 9 from each side.
   $x = -6$ Simplify.
The solution is -6.

b. $x - 5 = 2$ Write original equation.
   $x - 5 + 5 = 2 + 5$ Use addition property of equality. Add 5 to each side.
   $x = 7$ Simplify.
The solution is 7.

c. $x + 4.1 = 6$ Write original equation.
   $x + 4.1 - 4.1 = 6 - 4.1$ Subtract 4.1 from each side.
   $x = 1.9$ Simplify.
The solution is 1.9.

BENCHMARK 1
(Chapters 1 and 2)

PRACTICE **Use addition or subtraction to solve the equation.**

4. $x + 5 = 4$ **5.** $c - 3 = 8$ **6.** $t + 6 = 10$

3. Solve an Equation Using Multiplication or Division

EXAMPLE **Use multiplication or division to solve the equation.**

a. $\dfrac{x}{6} = 3$ **b.** $-7x = -49$ **c.** $-\dfrac{3}{8}x = 5$

Solution:

a. $\dfrac{x}{6} = 3$ Write original equation.

$6 \cdot \dfrac{x}{6} = 6 \cdot 3$ Multiply each side by 6.

$x = 18$ Simplify.

The solution is 18.

b. $-7x = -49$ Write original equation.

$\dfrac{-7x}{-7} = \dfrac{-49}{-7}$ Divide each side by -7.

$x = 7$ Simplify.

The solution is 7.

c. $-\dfrac{3}{8}x = 5$ Write original equation.

Recall that the product of a number and its *reciprocal* is 1.

$-\dfrac{8}{3}\left(-\dfrac{3}{8}x\right) = -\dfrac{8}{3}(5)$ Multiply each side by the reciprocal $-\dfrac{8}{3}$.

$x = -\dfrac{40}{3}$ Simplify.

The solution is $-\dfrac{40}{3}$.

PRACTICE **Use multiplication or division to solve the equation.**

7. $\dfrac{r}{10} = 2$ **8.** $4q = 32$ **9.** $\dfrac{a}{9} = -3$

4. Solve a Two-Step Equation

Vocabulary **Order of operations** The rules for evaluating an expression involving more than one operation.

EXAMPLE **Solve the equation.**

a. $7x + 1 = 4$ **b.** $\dfrac{x}{5} - 10 = 20$

Solution:

a. $7x + 1 = 4$ Write original equation.

$7x + 1 - 1 = 4 - 1$ Subtract 1 from each side.

$7x = 3$ Simplify.

$\dfrac{7x}{7} = \dfrac{3}{7}$ Divide each side by 7.

$x = \dfrac{3}{7}$ Simplify.

The solution is $\dfrac{3}{7}$.

BENCHMARK 1
(Chapters 1 and 2)

b. $\quad \frac{x}{5} - 10 = 20$ **Write original equation.**

$\frac{x}{5} - 10 + 10 = 20 + 10$ **Add 10 to each side.**

$\frac{x}{5} = 30$ **Simplify.**

$5 \cdot \frac{x}{5} = 5 \cdot 30$ **Multiply each side by 5.**

$x = 150$ **Simplify.**

The solution is 150.

PRACTICE   **Solve the equation.**

10. $3 + 4x = 11$ **11.** $7.5a - 10 = -32.5$ **12.** $\frac{t}{8} + 6 = 3$

5. Solve Multi-Step Equations

EXAMPLE   **Solve $4x + 3(x - 5) = -12$.**

Solution:

Distributive Property:
$a(b + c) = ab + ac$
$a(b - c) = ab - ac$

$4x + 3(x - 5) = -12$ **Write original equation.**

$4x + 3x - 15 = -12$ **Eliminate the parentheses by using the distributive property.**

$7x - 15 = -12$ **Combine like terms.**

$7x - 15 + 15 = -12 + 15$ **Add 15 to each side.**

$7x = 3$ **Simplify.**

$\frac{7x}{7} = \frac{3}{7}$ **Divide each side by 7.**

$x = \frac{3}{7}$ **Simplify.**

The solution is $\frac{3}{7}$.

PRACTICE   **Solve the equation.**

13. $-2(4a + 5) - 6a = 10$ **14.** $6 + 3(n - 7) = 12$ **15.** $\frac{2}{3}(6g + 1) + \frac{1}{3} = -19$

6. Solve Equations with Variables on Both Sides

EXAMPLE   **Solve $x - 4 = 3x + 8$.**

Solution:

You could also begin solving the equation by adding 4 to each side to obtain $x = 3x + 12$. You will get the same solution when you finish solving for x.

$x - 4 = 3x + 8$ **Write original equation.**

$x - 4 - 3x = 3x + 8 - 3x$ **Subtract 3x from each side.**

$-2x - 4 = 8$ **Simplify each side.**

$-2x - 4 + 4 = 8 + 4$ **Add 4 to each side.**

$-2x = 12$ **Simplify.**

$\frac{-2x}{-2} = \frac{12}{-2}$ **Divide each side by -2.**

$x = -6$ **Simplify.**

The solution is -6.

BENCHMARK 1
(Chapters 1 and 2)

PRACTICE **Solve the equation.**

16. $8t - 10 = 5 + 3t$ **17.** $-9 - 4h = -2h + 3$ **18.** $12d + 4 = 6 - d$

7. Identify the Number of Solutions to an Equation

Vocabulary **Identity** An equation that is true for all values of the variable.

EXAMPLE **Solve the equation, if possible.**

a. $-8x = -4(2x + 1)$ **b.** $-5x - 15 = -5(x + 3)$

Solution:

An equation can have *one* solution, *no* solution, or *all real numbers* as solutions.

a. $-8x = -4(2x + 1)$ Write original equation.

$-8x = -8x - 4$ Distributive property

$-8x + 8x = -8x - 4 + 8x$ Add 8*x* to each side.

$0 = -4$ ✘   Simplify.

The statement $0 = -4$ is not true, so the equation has no solution.

b. $-5x - 15 = -5(x + 3)$ Write original equation.

$-5x - 15 = -5x - 15$ Distributive property

The statement $-5x - 15 = -5x - 15$ is true for all values of *x*. So the equation is an identity, and the solution is all real numbers.

PRACTICE **Solve the equation, if possible.**

19. $7(3s - 3) = 3(7s - 7)$ **20.** $-6 + 3(v - 9) = 6v + 27$

21. $6a + 1 = 2(3a - 1)$

Quiz

Use addition or subtraction to solve the equation.

1. $w + 3.6 = 8.9$ **2.** $p - 7.2 = -5$ **3.** $v + 12 = -3$

Use multiplication or division to solve the equation.

4. $5n = -6$ **5.** $\dfrac{g}{2.1} = 5$ **6.** $1.2z = 8.4$

Solve the equation.

7. $9x - 2 = 0$ **8.** $-4 + \dfrac{b}{2.5} = 40$

9. $24 = \dfrac{v}{6} - 3$ **10.** $9y + 5(y - 9) = 39$

11. $-c + 4(8 - c) = -43$ **12.** $\dfrac{1}{4}m - \left(\dfrac{3}{4}m + 2\right) = 8$

13. $\dfrac{1}{2}n + 4 = -\dfrac{3}{2}n - 18$ **14.** $4.3 + 2.3r = 7.1 - 1.9r$

15. $z - 26 = 5z - 36$

Solve the equation, if possible.

16. $4(b - 5) = 5(b - 4)$ **17.** $8p - 12 = -4(-2p + 3)$

18. $5(k + 3) - k = 3k + 5$

BENCHMARK 1
(Chapters 1 and 2)

E. Proportion and Percent Problems

The comparison of two quantities by division is called a *ratio*. The following examples illustrate how to write and use ratios.

1. Write a Ratio

EXAMPLE

Kim has a jar containing 45 pennies, 18 nickels, 30 dimes, and 42 quarters. Write the specified ratio in simplest form.

The *ratio* of two quantities *a* and *b* can be written in three ways:
a to *b*, *a* : *b*, or $\frac{a}{b}$.

a. number of nickels to number of pennies

b. number of quarters to number of dimes

c. number of pennies to total number of coins

Solution:

a. $\dfrac{\text{nickels}}{\text{pennies}} = \dfrac{18}{45}$

$= \dfrac{2}{5}$

b. $\dfrac{\text{quarters}}{\text{dimes}} = \dfrac{42}{30}$

$= \dfrac{7}{5}$

c. $\dfrac{\text{pennies}}{\text{total}} = \dfrac{45}{45 + 18 + 30 + 42}$

$= \dfrac{45}{135} = \dfrac{1}{3}$

PRACTICE

On his last report card, Jay earned 2 A's, 3 B's, and 1 C. Write the specified ratio in simplest form.

1. the number of A's to the number of B's

2. the number of C's to the number of A's and B's

3. the number of B's to the total number of grades

A school band orders t-shirts. They order 12 smalls, 10 mediums, and 15 larges. Write the specified ratio in simplest form.

4. the number of smalls to the total number of t-shirts

5. the number of mediums to the number of larges

6. the number of larges and smalls to the number of mediums

2. Solve a Proportion

Vocabulary

Proportion An equation showing that two ratios are equivalent.

EXAMPLE

Solve the proportion $\frac{2}{3} = \frac{x}{15}$.

Solution:

$\dfrac{2}{3} = \dfrac{x}{15}$ **Write original proportion.**

$15 \cdot \dfrac{2}{3} = 15 \cdot \dfrac{x}{15}$ **Multiply each side by 15.**

$\dfrac{30}{3} = x$ **Simplify.**

$10 = x$ **Divide.**

BENCHMARK 1
(Chapters 1 and 2)

PRACTICE **Solve the proportion.**

7. $\dfrac{7}{42} = \dfrac{t}{84}$
8. $\dfrac{5}{6} = \dfrac{k}{72}$
9. $\dfrac{a}{65} = \dfrac{6}{39}$

10. $\dfrac{v}{3} = \dfrac{85}{51}$
11. $\dfrac{8}{20} = \dfrac{n}{15}$
12. $\dfrac{q}{54} = \dfrac{8}{36}$

3. Use the Cross Products Property

Vocabulary **Cross product** The product of the numerator of one ratio in a proportion and the denominator of the other ratio in the proportion.

EXAMPLE **Solve the proportion $\dfrac{2}{5} = \dfrac{x}{20}$.**

Solution:

Cross Products Property: The cross products of a proportion are equal.

$\dfrac{2}{5} = \dfrac{x}{20}$ — Write original proportion.

$2 \cdot 20 = 5 \cdot x$ — Cross products property

$40 = 5x$ — Simplify.

$8 = x$ — Divide each side by 5.

PRACTICE **Use the cross products property to solve the proportion.**

13. $\dfrac{y}{12} = \dfrac{19}{4}$
14. $\dfrac{15}{35} = \dfrac{p}{63}$
15. $\dfrac{13}{36} = \dfrac{65}{w}$

16. $\dfrac{7}{30} = \dfrac{196}{m-5}$
17. $\dfrac{5}{8} = \dfrac{n}{n+9}$
18. $\dfrac{18}{v-1} = \dfrac{48}{3v-5}$

Quiz

A shelter has 24 cats, 18 dogs, and 3 birds. Write each ratio in simplest form.

1. the number of dogs to the total number of animals

2. the number of dogs to the number of cats

3. the number of birds to the number of cats and dogs

Solve the proportion.

4. $\dfrac{48}{92} = \dfrac{8}{n}$
5. $\dfrac{84}{d} = \dfrac{70}{25}$
6. $\dfrac{20}{24} = \dfrac{3a}{90}$

7. $\dfrac{76}{d} = \dfrac{19}{13}$
8. $\dfrac{2}{7} = \dfrac{46}{s-2}$
9. $\dfrac{18}{7x+3} = \dfrac{3}{x+2}$

BENCHMARK 1
(Chapters 1 and 2)

F. Rewriting Equations in Two or More Variables

A literal equation describes the relationship between two or more variables. The equation can be rewritten, or "solved," to isolate any one of the variables. The following examples show how to solve and use literal equations.

1. Solve a Literal Equation

Vocabulary **Literal equation** An equation, such as a formula, with two or more variables where the coefficients and constants have been replaced by letters.

EXAMPLE **Solve $y = mx + b$ for m.**

Solution:

Remember that inverse operations apply to variables as well as to constants.

$y = mx + b$	Write original equation.
$y - b = mx$	Subtract b from each side.
$\dfrac{y - b}{x} = m$	Assume $x \neq 0$. Divide each side by x.

PRACTICE **Solve the literal equation for the specified variable.**

1. $I = Prt$ for P
2. $A = \pi r^2$ for r
3. $F + V = E + 2$ for V
4. $V = \ell w h$ for w
5. $V = \dfrac{1}{3}\pi r^2 h$ for h
6. $A = \dfrac{1}{2}(b_1 + b_2)h$ for b_1

2. Use the Solution to a Literal Equation

EXAMPLE **Use the solution to the literal equation from the example in Part 1 to solve $14 = m \cdot 6 - 4$.**

Solution:

After solving a literal equation, you can use unit analysis to check your work.

$\dfrac{y - b}{x} = m$	Solution of literal equation.
$\dfrac{14 - (-4)}{6} = m$	Substitute 14 for y, 6 for x, and -4 for b.
$3 = m$	Simplify.

PRACTICE **Solve the given formula for the unknown variable. Then use the solution to answer the question.**

7. The density d of a substance is given by $d = \dfrac{m}{V}$, where m is the mass in grams (g) and V is volume in cubic centimeters (cm³). A scientist completely fills a beaker with 28 g of a substance that has density 0.4375 g/cm³. What is the beaker's volume?

8. The strength s of a radio signal is given by $s = \dfrac{1600}{d^2}$, where d is the distance in miles from the transmitter. If s is 100, how far are you from the transmitter?

BENCHMARK 1
(Chapters 1 and 2)

9. A roller coaster car goes down a hill and then makes a loop. The velocity v of the car at the top of the loop is $v = 8\sqrt{h - 2r}$, where h is the hill's height and r is the loop's radius. If v is 32 ft/s and r is 15 ft, how tall is the hill?

3. Rewrite an Equation

EXAMPLE

Remember to first isolate the *term* containing the dependent variable. Then multiply or divide to isolate the *variable*.

Write $3x - 5y = 15$ so that y is a function of x.

Solution:

$3x - 5y = 15$	Write original equation.
$-5y = 15 - 3x$	Subtract $3x$ from each side.
$y = -3 + \dfrac{3}{5}x$	Divide each side by -5.

PRACTICE

Write the equation so that y is a function of x.

10. $2x - y = 10$ 11. $8 + 3y = -4x$ 12. $9y + 27 = -x$

13. $\dfrac{3}{4}y - 2x = 12$ 14. $5x + \dfrac{2}{5}y = 30$ 15. $-24 - 16y = 8x$

Quiz

Solve the literal equation for the specified variable.

1. $P = 4\ell$ for ℓ 2. $V = \pi r^2 h$ for h

3. $s = \dfrac{1}{2}(a + b + c)$ for a 4. $S = \pi r\ell + \pi r^2$ for ℓ

5. $h = -16t^2 + vt + c$ for v 6. $S = 2\ell w + 2wh + 2\ell h$ for w

Solve the given formula for the unknown variable. Then use the solution to answer the question.

7. For an electrical circuit, $I = \sqrt{\dfrac{P}{R}}$ gives the relationship between amperes of current I, watts of power P, and ohms of resistance R. For a certain circuit, I is 5 amperes and P is 75 watts. What is the circuit's resistance?

8. The sum s of the interior angles of an n-sided polygon is $s = (n - 2)180$. If the sum of the interior angles of a polygon is 2340, how many sides does it have?

9. The formula $e = \dfrac{c - \sqrt{c}}{c}$ gives the efficiency e of a car's engine. The variable c is the engine's compression ratio. If an engine has $e = 0.75$, what is the compression ratio?

Write the equation so that y is a function of x.

10. $6y - 3x = -12$ 11. $3x + 7y = 14$ 12. $7 - 3y = 21x$

13. $-4x - 5y = 9$ 14. $2 + 3y = -8x$ 15. $-4y + 36 = -24x$

BENCHMARK 2
(Chapters 3 and 4)

A. Graphing Linear Equations

The x-axis and y-axis divide a coordinate plane into four equal parts called **quadrants**. The quadrants are labeled with roman numerals I, II, III, and IV, moving counter-clockwise from the upper right quadrant. Each point in a coordinate plane has a unique ordered pair (x, y) that describes the point's location with respect to the origin $(0, 0)$.

The **solution** of an equation is the set of all ordered pairs (x, y) that make the equation a true statement. The graph of an equation is a graph of all the ordered pairs that make up the solution of the equation.

1. Plot Points in a Coordinate Plane

EXAMPLE   **Plot each point and describe its location.**

   a. $P(-4, -1)$ **b.** $Q(3, -4)$ **c.** $R(-2, 0)$ **d.** $S(0, -3)$

Solution:

Another name for the x-coordinate is *abscissa*.
Another name for the y-coordinate is *ordinate*.

   a. Start at the origin. Move 4 units left, then 1 unit down. Point P is in Quadrant III.

   b. Start at the origin. Move 3 units right, then 4 units down. Point Q is in Quadrant IV.

   c. Start at the origin. Move 2 units left. Point R is on the x-axis.

   d. Start at the origin. Move 3 units down. Point P is on the y-axis.

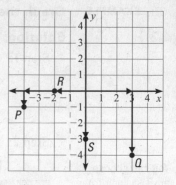

PRACTICE   **Plot each point and describe its location.**

   1. $A(3, 5)$ **2.** $B(-4, 0)$ **3.** $C(-1, 4)$

   4. $D(0, -1)$ **5.** $E(-2, -3)$ **6.** $F(1, -4)$

2. Identify Solutions to Equations in Two Variables

EXAMPLE   **Tell whether the ordered pair is a solution of the equation.**

   a. $x + 2y = 8$; $(-4, 6)$ **b.** $5x - 2y = 10$; $(2, 1)$

Solution:

   a. $x + 2y = 8$ **Write original equation.**

            $(-4) + 2(6) \stackrel{?}{=} 8$ **Substitute −4 for x and 6 for y.**

            $8 = 8 \checkmark$ **Simplify.**

       $(-4, 6)$ is a solution.

BENCHMARK 2
(Chapters 3 and 4)

BENCHMARK 2

A. Graphing Linear Equations

b. $5x - 2y = 10$ Write original equation.

$5(2) - 2(1) \overset{?}{=} 10$ Substitute 2 for x and 1 for y.

$8 \neq 10 \, ✗$ Simplify.

(2, 1) is not a solution.

PRACTICE   **Tell whether the ordered pair is a solution of the equation.**

7. $-2x + 3y = 4; \left(0, \frac{4}{3}\right)$ **8.** $-8 = y; (-5, -8)$

9. $3x - 4y = -1; (-3, -4)$ **10.** $x = -2; (-1, -2)$

11. $y - 5x = -3; (-2, -13)$ **12.** $-4y + 2x = 0; \left(-\frac{1}{2}, \frac{1}{4}\right)$

3. Graph an Equation Using a Table

EXAMPLE   **Graph the equation $-3x + y = 1$.**

Solution:

Step 1: Solve the equation for y:

$$-3x + y = 1$$

$$y = 3x + 1$$

Step 2: Make a table by choosing a few values for x and finding the values of y.

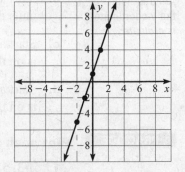

You can choose any (x, y) pair from the graph and substitute it in the equation to make a true statement.

x	-2	-1	0	1	2
y	-5	-2	1	4	7

Step 3: Plot the points. Notice that the points appear to lie on a line.

Step 4: Connect the points by drawing a line through them. Use arrows to indicate that the graph goes on without end.

PRACTICE   **Graph the equation.**

13. $x + y = 3$ **14.** $y - 2x = -1$ **15.** $-3x + 2y = 2$

16. $x - 3y = 3$ **17.** $4y - 3x = 8$ **18.** $2y - 5x = 0$

4. Graph Horizontal and Vertical Lines

Vocabulary   **Linear equation** An equation that can be written in the form $Ax + By = C$, where A, B, and C are real numbers and A and B are not both equal to zero. The graph of a linear equation is a straight line. When $A = 0$, the graph of the linear equation is a horizontal line. When $B = 0$, the graph of the linear equation is a vertical line.

BENCHMARK 2
(Chapters 3 and 4)

EXAMPLE

Graph the equation.

a. $y = -3$ **b.** $x = 1$

Solution:

All the solutions of $y = -3$ are ordered pairs in the form $(x, -3)$.

a. Notice that x can be any real number, but that y is always -3. The graph of the equation $y = -3$ is a horizontal line 3 units below the x-axis.

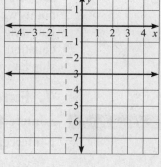

b. Notice that x will always be 1, but that y can be any real number. The graph of the equation $x = 1$ is a vertical line 1 unit to the right of the y-axis.

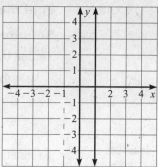

PRACTICE   **Graph the equation.**

19. $x = -5$ **20.** $y = 1$ **21.** $2y = -3$

22. $2x - 1 = 0$ **23.** $x - 3 = 0$ **24.** $y + 2 = 0$

Quiz

Plot each point and describe its location.

1. $A(4, -7)$ **2.** $B(-9, -2)$ **3.** $C(0, 7)$

4. $D(1, 3)$ **5.** $E(-6, 0)$ **6.** $F(-4, 8)$

Tell whether the ordered pair is a solution of the equation.

7. $-5 = y; (5, -5)$ **8.** $-x + 4y = 4; (4, 5)$ **9.** $-8y + 4x = 0; \left(-2, -\frac{1}{4}\right)$

10. $y - 2x = -6; \left(\frac{1}{2}, -5\right)$ **11.** $x = -9; (1, -9)$ **12.** $3x - 7y = -4; (1, 1)$

Graph the equation.

13. $x - y = -2$ **14.** $y + 3x = -4$ **15.** $-5x + 3y = 2$

16. $y = -7$ **17.** $-3y - 2x = 9$ **18.** $x = 8$

19. $4y - 6x = 0$ **20.** $3 = -x$ **21.** $2y + 5 = -3$

BENCHMARK 2
(Chapters 3 and 4)

B. Slope-Intercept Form and Direct Variation

For any two points, there is one and only one line that contains both points. This fact can help you graph a linear equation. Many times, it will be convenient to use the points where the line crosses the x-axis and y-axis. These points are the **intercepts**. Knowing how steep the line is, or the **slope** of the line, also can help you graph a linear equation. If the graph of a linear equation passes through the origin (0, 0), the relationship between x and y is called a **direct variation**.

1. Find the Intercepts of the Graph of an Equation

Vocabulary   **x-intercept** The x-coordinate of the point where a graph intersects the x-axis.

y-intercept The y-coordinate of the point where a graph intersects the y-axis.

EXAMPLE   **Find the x-intercept and the y-intercept of the graph of $3x + 4y = 12$.**

Solution:

To find the x-intercept, substitute 0 for y and solve for x.

$3x + 4y = 12$	Write original equation.
$3x + 4(0) = 12$	Substitute 0 for y.
$x = \dfrac{12}{3} = 4$	Solve for x.

To find the y-intercept, substitute 0 for x and solve for y.

$3x + 4y = 12$	Write original equation.
$3(0) + 4y = 12$	Substitute 0 for x.
$y = \dfrac{12}{4} = 3$	Solve for y.

The x-intercept is 4. The y-intercept is 3.

Remember that the x- and y-intercepts are numbers, NOT ordered pairs.

PRACTICE   **Find the x-intercept and the y-intercept of the graph of the equation.**

1. $x + y = -6$ **2.** $-3y + 8 = -12x$ **3.** $4.5x + 0.5y = 9$

4. $-7y = 14x$ **5.** $-15 + 10y = 60x$ **6.** $3 - 18x = -6y$

2. Find the Slope of a Line

Vocabulary   **Slope** Describes how quickly a line rises or falls as it moves from left to right. Slope is the ratio m of the vertical change between two points on the line to the horizontal change between the same two points.

For points (x_1, y_1) and (x_2, y_2), $m = \dfrac{y_2 - y_1}{x_2 - x_1}$.

EXAMPLE   **Find the slope of the line that passes through the points.**

a. $(1, 5)$ and $(4, 6)$ **b.** $(-5, 7)$ and $(3, -1)$

c. $(-2, 7)$ and $(8, 7)$ **d.** $(6, -8)$ and $(6, 2)$

BENCHMARK 2
(Chapters 3 and 4)

Solution:

Think of (x_1, y_1) as "the coordinates of the first point" and (x_2, y_2) as "the coordinates of the second point." Be sure to subtract the x- and y-coordinates in the same order.

a. Let $(x_1, y_1) = (1, 5)$ and $(x_2, y_2) = (4, 6)$.

$m = \dfrac{y_2 - y_1}{x_2 - x_1}$ **Write formula for slope.**

$\quad = \dfrac{6 - 5}{4 - 1} = \dfrac{1}{3}$ **Substitute and simplify.**

b. Let $(x_1, y_1) = (-5, 7)$ and $(x_2, y_2) = (3, -1)$.

$m = \dfrac{y_2 - y_1}{x_2 - x_1}$ **Write formula for slope.**

$\quad = \dfrac{-1 - 7}{3 - (-5)} = \dfrac{-8}{8} = -1$ **Substitute and simplify.**

c. Let $(x_1, y_1) = (-2, 7)$ and $(x_2, y_2) = (8, 7)$.

$m = \dfrac{y_2 - y_1}{x_2 - x_1}$ **Write formula for slope.**

$\quad = \dfrac{7 - 7}{8 - (-2)} = \dfrac{0}{10} = 0$ **Substitute and simplify.**

The slope is 0. The line is horizontal.

d. Let $(x_1, y_1) = (6, -8)$ and $(x_2, y_2) = (6, 2)$.

$m = \dfrac{y_2 - y_1}{x_2 - x_1}$ **Write formula for slope.**

$\quad = \dfrac{2 - (-8)}{6 - 6} = \dfrac{10}{0}$ **Substitute. Division by 0 is undefined.**

The slope is undefined. The line is vertical.

PRACTICE   **Find the slope of the line that passes through the points.**

7. $(6, -9)$ and $(-9, 6)$ **8.** $(4, 2)$ and $(4, 0)$

9. $(-11, 8)$ and $(13, 5)$ **10.** $(-1, -7)$ and $(1, -7)$

11. $(2.5, -5)$ and $(5.5, -9)$ **12.** $(-3, -5)$ and $(-2, 0)$

3. Graph an Equation Using Slope-Intercept Form

Vocabulary   **Slope-intercept form** A linear equation in the form $y = mx + b$, where m is the slope and b is the y-intercept of the graph of the equation.

EXAMPLE   **Graph the equation $-x + 2y = 4$.**

Solution:

If you can substitute the coordinates of the second point in the original equation and get a true statement, then your graph is correct.

Step 1: **Rewrite** the equation in slope-intercept form.

$\quad y = \dfrac{1}{2}x + 2$

Step 2: **Identify** the slope and the y-intercept.

$\quad m = \dfrac{1}{2}$ and $b = 2$.

Step 2: **Plot** the point that corresponds to the y-intercept, $(0, 2)$.

Step 4: **Use** the slope to find another point on the line. Draw a line through the two points.

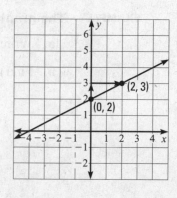

BENCHMARK 2
(Chapters 3 and 4)

PRACTICE   **Graph the equation.**

13. $y = -\dfrac{2}{5}x + 7$ 14. $-3x = 4y + 8$ 15. $3x - 3y = 6$

16. $y = -4$ 17. $-14x - 7y = 21$ 18. $1.5y - 6x - 12 = 0$

4. Identify Direct Variation Equations

Vocabulary   **Direct variation** An equation in the form $y = ax$, where $a \neq 0$, represents direct variation. The variable y *varies directly* with x.

Constant of variation The constant a in the direct variation equation $y = ax$.

EXAMPLE   **Tell whether the equation represents direct variation. If so, identify the constant of variation.**

   a. $6x - 4y = 0$ **b.** $x + y = 8$

Solution:

Try to rewrite the equation in the form $y = ax$.

   a. $6x - 4y = 0$ **Write original equation.**

          $-4y = -6x$ **Subtract $-6x$ from each side.**

          $y = \dfrac{3}{2}x$ **Simplify.**

   Because the equation $6x - 4y = 0$ can be rewritten in the form $y = ax$,

   it represents direct variation. The constant of variation is $\dfrac{3}{2}$.

   b. $x + y = 8$ **Write original equation.**

          $y = -x + 8$ **Subtract x from each side.**

   Because the equation $x + y = 8$ cannot be rewritten in the form $y = ax$, it does not represent direct variation.

PRACTICE   **Tell whether the equation represents direct variation. If so, identify the constant of variation.**

19. $y = -\dfrac{7}{8}x$ 20. $x + 4 = 16y$ 21. $9y = 5x$

22. $x = -47y$ 23. $-3 + x + 7 = -y + 4$ 24. $13 = 26x$

5. Write and Use a Direct Variation Equation

EXAMPLE   **The graph of a direct variation equation is shown.**

   a. Write the direct variation equation.

   b. Find the value of y when $x = 36$.

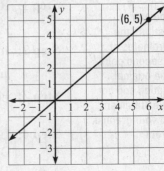

BENCHMARK 2
(Chapters 3 and 4)

Check the sign of the constant of variation in your equation. If the graph of $y = ax$ passes through Quadrants I and III, the constant should be positive. If the graph of $y = ax$ passes through Quadrants II and IV, the constant should be negative.

Solution:

a. Because y varies directly x, the equation has the form $y = ax$. Use the fact that $y = 5$ when $x = 6$ to find a.

$y = ax$ **Write direct variation equation.**

$5 = a(6)$ **Substitute.**

$\dfrac{5}{6} = a$ **Solve for a.**

A direct variation equation that relates x and y is $y = \dfrac{5}{6}x$.

b. When $x = 36$, $y = \dfrac{5}{6}(36) = 30$.

PRACTICE

Write the direct variation equation that passes through the given point. Then find the value of y for the given x.

25. $(3, -1); x = 12$ **26.** $(-4, -8); x = 32$ **27.** $(-6, 3); x = 18$

28. $(9, 2); x = 27$ **29.** $(-5, 7); x = 100$ **30.** $(-2, -1); x = 74$

Quiz

Find the *x*-intercept and the *y*-intercept of the graph of the equation.

  1. $-21 + 14y = 84x$ **2.** $-3 + x = 3y$ **3.** $3.2x + 0.8y = 4$

Find the slope of the line that passes through the points.

  4. $(8, -5)$ and $(-3, 4)$ **5.** $(1, 7)$ and $(-2, 7)$ **6.** $(-9, 7)$ and $(3, -5)$

Graph the equation.

  7. $y = x + 1$ **8.** $y = -2$ **9.** $4x - 6y = 12$

Does the equation represent direct variation? If so, find the constant of variation.

  10. $y = -\dfrac{4}{5}x$ **11.** $x + 3 = 9y$ **12.** $4y = 7x$

Write the direct variation equation that passes through the given point. Then find the value of y for the given x.

  13. $(2, -5); x = 20$ **14.** $(-3, -9); x = 43$ **15.** $(-4, 6); x = 64$

BENCHMARK 2
(Chapters 3 and 4)

C. Writing Linear Equations

You can describe a line with equations in three different forms. You can write these equations if you know the slope and y-intercept of the line, if you know the slope and a point on the line, or if you know two points on the line. The following examples illustrate these three different forms of the equation of a line and show how to find them.

1. Write an Equation in Slope-Intercept Form

Vocabulary   **Slope-intercept form**   The equation $y = mx + b$, for a line with slope m and y-intercept b.

EXAMPLE   **Write an equation of the line with a slope of $\frac{1}{3}$ and a y-intercept of -2.**

Solution:

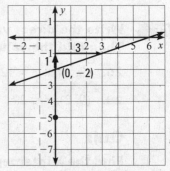

$y = mx + b$ Write slope-intercept form.

$y = \frac{1}{3}x - 2$ Substitute $\frac{1}{3}$ for m and -2 for b.

PRACTICE   **Write an equation of the line with the given slope and y-intercept.**

1. Slope is 6; y-intercept is -4.   **2.** Slope is -1; y-intercept is 3.

3. Slope is $\frac{3}{5}$; y-intercept is -5.   **4.** Slope is $\frac{2}{5}$; y-intercept is -3.

5. Slope is -4; y-intercept is 5.   **6.** Slope is $-\frac{1}{3}$; y-intercept is -2.

2. Write an Equation of a Line Given the Slope and a Point

EXAMPLE   **Write an equation of the line that passes through $(4, -3)$ and has a slope of -2.**

Solution:

Step 1:   **Identify** the slope. The slope is -2.

Step 2:   **Find** the y-intercept. Substitute the slope and the coordinates of the given point in $y = mx + b$. Solve for b.

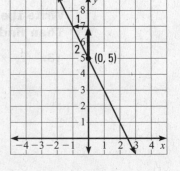

Make sure you don't switch the x and y values when you substitute.

$y = mx + b$ Write slope-intercept form.

$-3 = -2(4) + b$ Substitute -2 for m, 4 for x, and -3 for y.

$5 = b$ Solve for b.

BENCHMARK 2
(Chapters 3 and 4)

Step 3: **Write** an equation of the line.

$$y = mx + b$$ Write slope-intercept form.

$$y = -2x + 5$$ Substitute 2 for *m* and 5 for *b*.

PRACTICE   **Write an equation of the line that passes through the given point and has the given slope.**

7. $(-6, -2); m = \dfrac{4}{3}$ **8.** $(-1, 3); m = -\dfrac{1}{4}$

9. $(3, 4); m = -6$ **10.** $(5, -3); m = \dfrac{3}{2}$

11. $(-3, 6); m = -\dfrac{2}{3}$ **12.** $(-1, -4); m = 2$

3. Write an Equation of a Line Given Two Points

EXAMPLE   **Write an equation of the line shown.**

Solution:

Step 1: **Calculate** the slope using the formula.

$$m = \frac{y_2 - y_1}{x_2 - x_1} = \frac{2 - 6}{-3 - (-5)} = \frac{-4}{2} = -2$$

Step 2: **Find** the *y*-intercept. Use the point $(-5, 6)$.

$$y = mx + b$$ Write slope-intercept form.

$$6 = -2(-5) + b$$ Substitute 6 for *y*, −2 for *m*, and −5 for *x*.

$$6 - 10 = b$$ Solve for *b*.

$$-4 = b$$

You also could find *b* by substituting the *x* and *y* values from the other known point, $(-3, 2)$.

Step 3: **Write** an equation of the line.

$$y = mx + b$$ Write slope-intercept form.

$$y = -2x - 4$$ Substitute −2 for *m* and −4 for *b*.

PRACTICE   **Write an equation of the line shown.**

13.

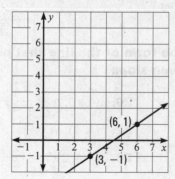

14.

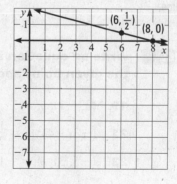

BENCHMARK 2
(Chapters 3 and 4)

15.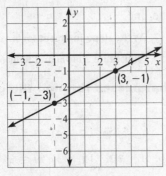

16.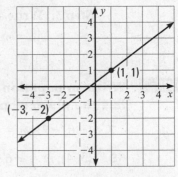

17.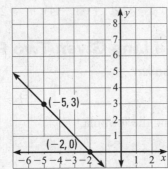

18.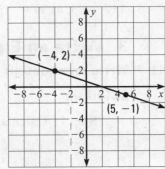

4. Write an Equation in Point-Slope Form

Vocabulary **Point-slope form** The equation $y - y_1 = m(x - x_1)$, for the nonvertical line through a given point (x_1, y_1) with slope m.

EXAMPLE **Write an equation in point-slope form of the line that passes through the point (−2, 1) and has a slope of 2.**

Solution:

Notice that (x_1, y_1) is a point of the line, and that m is the slope of the line.

$y - y_1 = m(x - x_1)$ Write point-slope form.

$y - 1 = 2(x + 2)$ Substitute 1 for y_1, 2 for m, and −2 for x_1.

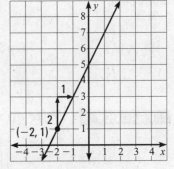

PRACTICE **Write an equation in point-slope form of the line that passes through the given point and has the given slope.**

19. $(3, -1); m = \dfrac{2}{3}$

20. $(4, 0); m = -\dfrac{1}{4}$

21. $(-3, -4); m = \dfrac{1}{2}$

22. $(1, 1); m = \dfrac{3}{4}$

23. $(-5, 3); m = -1$

24. $(-4, 2); m = -\dfrac{1}{3}$

Name _____ Date _____

BENCHMARK 2
(Chapters 3 and 4)

5. Write an Equation in Standard Form

Vocabulary **Standard form** The equation $Ax + By = C$, where A, B, and C are real numbers and A and B are not both zero.

EXAMPLE **Write an equation in standard form of the line shown.**

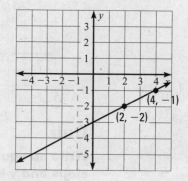

Solution:

Step 1: Calculate the slope.

$$m = \frac{y_2 - y_1}{x_2 - x_1} = \frac{-1 - (-2)}{4 - 2} = \frac{1}{2}$$

Step 2: Write an equation in point-slope form. Use $(2, -2)$.

$y - y_1 = m(x - x_1)$ **Write point-slope form.**

$y - (-2) = \frac{1}{2}(x - 2)$ **Substitute -2 for y_1, $\frac{1}{2}$ for m, and 2 for x_1.**

Step 3: Rewrite the equation in standard form.

$y + 2 = \frac{1}{2}x - 1$ **Apply the distributive property.**

$2y + 4 = x - 2$ **Multiply each term by 2.**

$-x + 2y = -6$ **Simplify. Collect variable terms on one side, constants on the other.**

PRACTICE **Write an equation in standard form of the line shown.**

25.

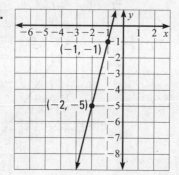

26.

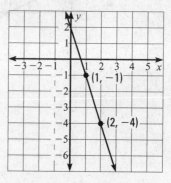

27.

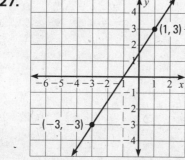

28.

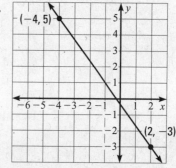

BENCHMARK 2
(Chapters 3 and 4)

29.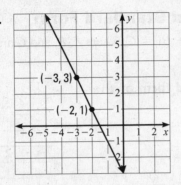

30.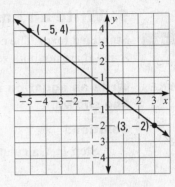

Quiz

Write an equation in slope-intercept form of the line with the given slope and *y*-intercept.

1. Slope is 4; *y*-intercept is 3.

2. Slope is -2; *y*-intercept is 1.

3. Slope is $\frac{5}{2}$; *y*-intercept is -4.

4. Slope is $-\frac{1}{3}$; *y*-intercept is -5.

Write an equation in the given form of the line that passes through the given point and has the given slope.

5. $(-3, -4)$; $m = \frac{1}{5}$

slope-intercept form

6. $(-2, 7)$; $m = -\frac{3}{4}$

point-slope form

7. $(1, 5)$; $m = -4$

point-slope form

Write equations in slope-intercept form and standard form of the line shown.

8.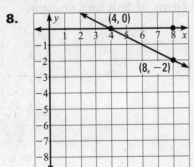

9.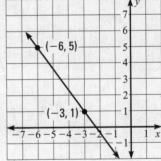

BENCHMARK 2
(Chapters 3 and 4)

D. Parallel and Perpendicular Lines

If two non-vertical lines in the same plane have the same slope, then they are parallel.
If their slopes are negative reciprocals, then they are perpendicular. The converse is
also true. If two non-vertical lines in the same plane are parallel, then they have the
same slope. If they are perpendicular, then their slopes are negative reciprocals.

1. Determine Whether Lines are Parallel or Perpendicular

Vocabulary   **Perpendicular lines** Lines in a plane that intersect to form a right (90°) angle.

EXAMPLE   **Determine which lines, if any, are parallel or perpendicular.**

Line a: $y = 4x - 1$ Line b: $-4x + y = 3$ Line c: $2x + 8y = 4$

Solution:

Step 1: **Write** each equation in slope-intercept form. Find the slopes of the lines.

Line a: The equation is in slope-intercept form. The slope is 4.

The product of a
non-zero slope m
and its negative
reciprocal is -1:
$m\left(-\dfrac{1}{m}\right) = -1$

Line b: $-4x + y = 3$
$y = 4x + 3$

Line c: $x + 4y = 4$
$y = -\dfrac{1}{4}x + 1$

Step 2: **Compare** the slopes. Line a and line b have slopes of 4,

so they are parallel. Line c has a slope of $-\dfrac{1}{4}$. $4\left(-\dfrac{1}{4}\right) = -1$,
so it is perpendicular to lines a and b.

PRACTICE   **Determine which lines, if any, are parallel or perpendicular.**

1. Line a: $y = \dfrac{3}{4}x + 2$ Line b: $4x - 3y = -3$ Line c: $3x - 4y = 20$

2. Line d: $x - 2y = 4$ Line e: $2x + y = 0$ Line f: $x + 2y = 3$

3. Line g: $5x + 7y = 7$ Line h: $y = \dfrac{7}{5}x + 3$ Line j: $7x - 5y = 2$

2. Write an Equation of a Parallel Line

EXAMPLE   **Write an equation of the line that passes through (1, −2) and is parallel
to the line $y = 5x + 2$.**

Solution:

Step 1: **Identify** the slope. The graph of the given equation has a slope of 5.
So, the parallel line through (1, −2) will also have a slope of 5.

Step 2: **Find** the y-intercept. Use the slope and the given point.

$y = mx + b$ Write slope-intercept form.

$-2 = 5(1) + b$ Substitute −2 for y, 5 for m, and 1 for x.

$-7 = b$ Solve for b.

BENCHMARK 2
(Chapters 3 and 4)

You can graph both lines to check your answer.

Step 3: **Write** an equation of the line in slope-intercept form.

$$y = mx + b$$ Write slope-intercept form.

$$y = 5x - 7$$ Substitute 5 for *m* and −7 for *b*.

PRACTICE **Write an equation of the line that passes through the given point and is parallel to the given line.**

4. $(-3, -1); y = \frac{4}{3}x + 1$

5. $(-8, 5); y = -\frac{1}{4}x - 2$

6. $(2, 3); y = -6x + 4$

7. $(2, 0); y = \frac{3}{2}x - 7$

8. $(-6, 4); y = -\frac{2}{3}x + 3$

9. $(-5, -2); y = 2x - 9$

3. Write an Equation of a Perpendicular Line

EXAMPLE **Write an equation of the line that passes through (4, 3) and is perpendicular to the line $y = 2x - 3$.**

Solution:

Step 1: **Identify** the slope. The graph of the given equation has a slope of 2. So, the slope of the perpendicular line through (4, 3) will be the negative reciprocal of 2, which is $-\frac{1}{2}$.

Step 2: **Find** the *y*-intercept. Use the slope and the given point.

$$y = mx + b$$ Write slope-intercept form.

$$3 = -\frac{1}{2}(4) + b$$ Substitute 3 for *y*, $-\frac{1}{2}$ for *m*, and 4 for *x*.

$$5 = b$$ Solve for *b*.

Step 3: **Write** an equation of the line in slope-intercept form.

$$y = mx + b$$ Write slope-intercept form.

$$y = -\frac{1}{2}x + 5$$ Substitute $-\frac{1}{2}$ for *m* and 5 for *b*.

PRACTICE **Write an equation of the line that passes through the given point and is perpendicular to the given line.**

10. $(-3, -2); y = \frac{3}{2}x + 2$

11. $(-6, 1); y = -\frac{3}{4}x - 1$

12. $(2, 5); y = -8x + 3$

13. $(4, 0); y = \frac{1}{3}x - 4$

14. $(4, 6); y = -\frac{2}{3}x + 3$

15. $(-8, -2); y = 2x - 6$

BENCHMARK 2
(Chapters 3 and 4)

Quiz

Determine which lines, if any, are parallel or perpendicular.

1. Line a: $y = -\frac{3}{2}x + 4$ Line b: $3x + 2y = 2$ Line c: $2x - 3y = 3$

2. Line d: $x + 3y = 9$ Line e: $y = 3x - 2$ Line f: $3x + y = 2$

3. Line g: $x + 4y = 2$ Line h: $x - 4y = 0$ Line j: $y = \frac{1}{4}x + 1$

Write an equation of the line that passes through the given point and is parallel to the given line.

4. $(8, 1)$; $y = \frac{3}{8}x$ **5.** $(-3, 3)$; $y = -\frac{2}{3}x - 5$ **6.** $(-5, -2)$; $y = 2x + 2$

7. $(-6, 2)$; $y = \frac{4}{3}x + 4$ **8.** $(-8, 0)$; $y = -\frac{1}{4}x - 3$ **9.** $(3, 2)$; $y = -5x + 1$

Write an equation of the line that passes through the given point and is perpendicular to the given line.

10. $(1, 7)$; $y = \frac{1}{3}x - 2$ **11.** $(6, 4)$; $y = -\frac{2}{3}x + 6$ **12.** $(-4, -3)$; $y = 2x - 7$

13. $(-6, 2)$; $y = \frac{3}{2}x + 5$ **14.** $(3, -1)$; $y = -\frac{3}{4}x - 8$ **15.** $(8, 2)$; $y = -4x + 1$

BENCHMARK 2
D. Parallel and Perpendicular

BENCHMARK 2
(Chapters 3 and 4)

E. Linear Models

Paired data graphed in a **scatter plot** may show a **positive correlation**, a **negative correlation**, or no correlation. If there is a positive or negative correlation, the data can be modeled by a **line of fit** drawn close to the points on the scatter plot. The equation of this line will be in the form $y = mx + b$. Using **linear regression**, you can find the line that best fits the data. This **best-fitting line** or its equation can be used to approximate data points between or beyond known data points.

1. Describe the Correlation of Data

Vocabulary   **Correlation** The relationship between paired data; If the value of y tends to increase as the value of x increases, the correlation is positive. If the value of y tends to decrease as the value of x increases, the correlation is negative.

Scatter plot A graph that shows the relationship, if any, between paired data.

EXAMPLE   **Describe the correlation, if any, of the data graphed in the scatter plot.**

a.
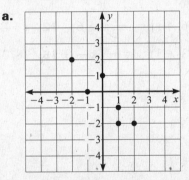

b.
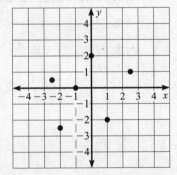

c.
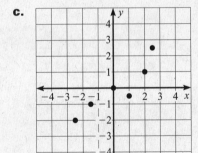

Solution:

a. The value of y decreases as the value of x increases: *negative* correlation.

b. There is no apparent relationship between the value of y and x: *no* correlation.

c. The value of y increases as the value of x increases: *positive* correlation.

Name _____   Date _____

BENCHMARK 2
(Chapters 3 and 4)

 PRACTICE   Describe the correlation, if any, of the data graphed in the scatter plot.

1.
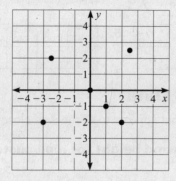

2.
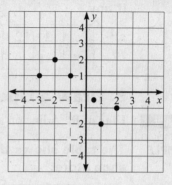

3.
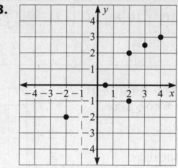

2. Make a Scatter Plot

EXAMPLE   Tracy is training for a swim race. The table shows her fastest time from each practice session for six days.

Practice day	1	2	3	4	5	6
Fastest time (min)	6.6	6.5	6.5	6.3	6.2	6.0

a. Make a scatter plot of the data.

b. *Describe* the correlation of the data.

Solution:

Notice that a negative correlation is not always an "undesirable" outcome.

a. Treat the data as ordered pairs. Let x represent the training day and let y represent the fastest time each day. Plot the ordered pairs as points in a coordinate plane.

b. The scatter plot shows a negative correlation. The more Tracy trains, the less time she takes to finish the race.

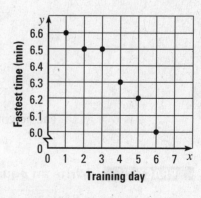

BENCHMARK 2
(Chapters 3 and 4)

PRACTICE Make a scatter plot of the data in the table. Describe the correlation, if any.

4.

x	2	2	3	5	5	6
y	−1	0	2	3	6	6

5.

x	−3	−2	−1	−1	0	2
y	1	0	−2	−3	−3	−4

3. Draw a Line of Fit to Data

Vocabulary **Line of fit** A line on a scatter plot that appears to fit the data closely.

EXAMPLE The table shows the shoe size and height for nine customers of a men's shoe store.

Shoe Size	9	9	10	$10\frac{1}{2}$	11	11	$11\frac{1}{2}$	12	12
Height (in.)	67	69	68	70	72	73	75	74	76

Write an equation that models the height of a customer as a function of his shoe size.

Solution:

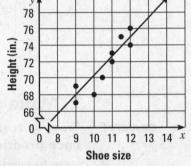

Step 1: **Make** a scatter plot of the data. Let x represent shoe size. Let y represent height.

Step 2: **Decide** whether the data can be modeled by a line. As shoe size increases, height tends to increase, so the scatter plot shows a positive correlation. You can fit a line to the data.

A line of fit and its equation model the trend in the data.

Step 3: **Draw** a line of fit. The line should be close to the data points, with about the same number of points above and below the line.

Step 4: **Write** an equation using two points on the line. Use (9, 68) and (12, 75).

Find the slope of the line. $m = \frac{y_2 - y_1}{x_2 - x_1} = \frac{75 - 68}{12 - 9} = \frac{7}{3}$

Find the y-intercept of the line. Use the point (9, 68).

$y = mx + b$ **Write slope-intercept form.**

$68 = \frac{7}{3}(9) + b$ **Substitute 68 for y, $\frac{7}{3}$ for m, and 9 for x.**

$47 = b$ **Solve for b.**

The height in inches y of a customer can be modeled by the function

$y = \frac{7}{3}x + 47$, where x is the customer's shoe size.

PRACTICE Write an equation that models y as a function of x.

6.

x	5	4	3	2	1	0
y	0	0	−2	−3	−4	−3

7.

x	0	0	1	1	2	2
y	−5	−3	−3	−1	0	2

BENCHMARK 2
(Chapters 3 and 4)

4. Interpolate Using an Equation

Vocabulary   **Linear interpolation** To use a line or its equation to estimate a value between two known values.

EXAMPLE   **Use the data about shoe store customer's sizes and heights to find the equation of the best-fitting line for the data. Then approximate the height of a customer who wears shoe size $9\frac{1}{2}$.**

Solution:

Step 1: Enter the data into lists on a graphing calculator. Make a scatter plot of the data. Let the x-values be shoe size and the y-values be height.

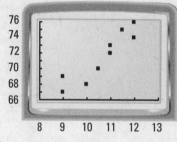

Step 2: Perform linear regression using the paired data. The equation of the best-fitting line is approximately $y = 2.6x + 44$.

Step 3: Find the value of y when $x = 9.5$.

$y = 2.6x + 44$ **Equation of best-fitting line**

$y = 2.6(9.5) + 44$ **Substitute 9.5 for x.**

$y \approx 68.7$ **Simplify.**

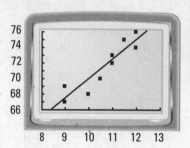

A customer who wears a size $9\frac{1}{2}$ shoe is probably about 68.7 inches tall.

PRACTICE   **Make a scatter plot of the data. Find the equation of the best-fitting line. Approximate the value of y for $x = 4$.**

8.

x	-5	-3	-1	1	3	5
y	4	3	1	0	-2	-3

9.

x	0	1	3	6	7	8
y	-2	-1	0	1	2	4

5. Extrapolate Using an Equation

Vocabulary   **Linear extrapolation** To use a line or its equation to estimate a value beyond the range of known values.

EXAMPLE   **Use the data about shoe store customer's sizes and heights to estimate the height of a customer who wears size 13.**

Solution:

Use the equation of the best-fitting line to find the value of y when $x = 13$.

$y = 2.6x + 44$

$y = 2.6(13) + 44 = 77.8$

A customer who wears a size 13 shoe is probably about 77.8 inches tall.

Name _____ Date _____

BENCHMARK 2
(Chapters 3 and 4)

PRACTICE Make a scatter plot of the data. Find the equation of the best-fitting line. Approximate the value of *y* for *x* = 7.

10.

x	−4	−3	0	0	2	5
y	2	2	1	0	−1	−4

11.

x	−2	−1	1	2	4	5
y	−5	−4	−1	0	0	3

Quiz

Describe the correlation, if any, of the data graphed in the scatter plot.

1.
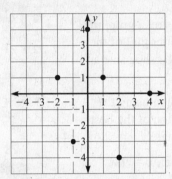

2.
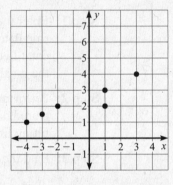

3.
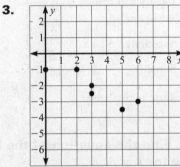

4. A bookstore is interested in the relationship between the number of rainy days in a month and the number of sales. The table shows data for six months.

	Apr	May	Jun	Jul	Aug	Sep
Rainy days	8	6	5	5	6	3
Sales	105	91	85	90	92	75

a. Make a scatter plot of the data.

b. Describe the correlation.

c. Draw a line of fit. Write the equation of the line.

d. Perform linear regression to find the equation of the best-fitting line.

e. Estimate the number of sales during a month with 4 rainy days. Estimate the number of sales during a month with 10 rainy days.

BENCHMARK 3
(Chapters 5 and 6)

A. Graphing Inequalities

An inequality is a statement that compares unequal quantities. A compound inequality is the intersection or union of two inequalities. The graph of an inequality is the set of points that represents all solutions of the inequality. The graph of an inequality in one variable is a line, line segment, or ray graphed on a number line. The graph of an inequality in two variables is a half-plane and boundary line graphed on a coordinate plane.

1. Graph an Inequality

EXAMPLE   **The least expensive book at the City Bookstore costs $2. Graph an inequality that describes prices of books at City Bookstore.**

Solution:

Let P represent the price of a book at City Bookstore. The value of P must be greater than or equal to 2. So, an inequality is $P \geq 2$.

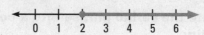

To graph an inequality in one variable, use an open circle for $<$ or $>$ and a closed circle for $\leq$ or $\geq$.

PRACTICE   **Graph an inequality that describes the situation.**

1. The shortest player on a basketball team is 74 inches tall.

2. A diver's depth is at least 30 feet below sea level.

3. A pitcher holds a maximum of 8 cups of water.

4. A computer has 162 megabytes of open storage space.

2. Write an Inequality Represented by a Graph

EXAMPLE   **Write an inequality represented by the graph.**

a.
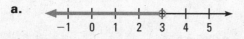

b.
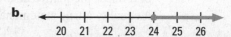

Solution:

a. The open circle means that 3 is NOT a solution of the inequality. Because the arrow points to the left, all numbers less than 3 are solutions.

The graph represents the inequality $x < 3$.

b. The closed circle means that 24 is a solution of the inequality. Because the arrow points to the right, all numbers greater than 24 also are solutions.

The graph represents the inequality $x \geq 24$.

PRACTICE   **Write an inequality represented by the graph.**

5.
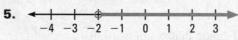

6.
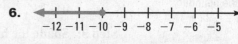

7.
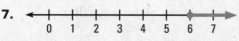

8.
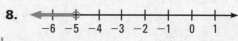

BENCHMARK 3
(Chapters 5 and 6)

3. Write and Graph Compound Inequalities

Vocabulary   **Compound inequality** Two inequalities joined by *and* or *or*. The graph of a compound inequality with *and* contains only the points that the graphs of the separate inequalities have in common. The graph of a compound inequality with *or* contains all the points on the graphs of the separate inequalities.

EXAMPLE   **Translate the verbal phrase into a compound inequality. Then graph the inequality.**

    a. All real numbers that are less than or equal to 7 *and* greater than 1.

    b. All real numbers that are greater than or equal to 4 *or* less than −4.

Solution:

    a. $1 < x \le 7$

    b. $x \ge 4 \ or \ x < -4$

 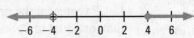

PRACTICE   **Translate the verbal phrase into a compound inequality. Then graph the inequality.**

    9. All real numbers that are greater than −3 *and* less than 0.

    10. All real numbers that are less than or equal to 2 *or* greater than or equal to 9.

    11. All real numbers that are less than 6 *and* greater than or equal to −1.

    12. All real numbers that are greater than or equal to 60 *or* less than 55.

4. Graph a Linear Inequality in Two Variables

Vocabulary   **Linear inequality in two variables** A statement that can be written in one of the following forms: $y > mx + b$; $y \ge mx + b$; $y < mx + b$; or $y \le mx + b$. The solution of a linear inequality in two variables is the set of ordered pairs (x, y) that makes the inequality a true statement.

EXAMPLE   **Graph the inequality $y < 2x + 1$.**

Solution:

Step 1: **Graph** the boundary line, $y = 2x + 1$. The inequality is <, so use a dashed line.

Step 2: **Test** a point NOT on the boundary line of the inequality. Test $(0, 0)$ in
$$y < 2x + 1.$$
$$0 \overset{?}{<} 2(0) + 1$$
$$0 < 1 \checkmark$$

Step 3: **Shade** the half-plane that contains $(0, 0)$, because $(0, 0)$ is a solution of the inequality.

Be sure that the point you test is not on the boundary line. In this example, you could not use (0, 1) because it is on the boundary line $y = 2x + 1$.

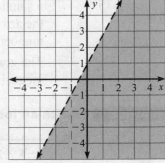

BENCHMARK 3
(Chapters 5 and 6)

EXAMPLE   **Graph the inequality $3x + 2y \geq 4$.**

Solution:

> **Step 1:** **Graph** the equation $3x + 2y = 4$.
> The inequality is $\geq$, so use a solid line.
>
> **Step 2:** **Test** $(1, 0)$ in $3x + 2y \geq 4$.
>
> $$3(1) + 2(0) \; / 4$$
> $$3 \overset{?}{\geq} 4 \; ✗$$
>
> **Step 3:** **Shade** the half-plane that does NOT
> contain $(1, 0)$, because $(1, 0)$ is NOT
> a solution of the inequality.

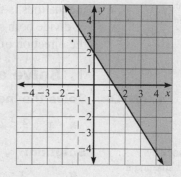

PRACTICE   **Graph the inequality.**

13. $y > -x + 3$ **14.** $2x - y \leq 2$ **15.** $y < 5x$

16. $-2x + 3y \leq -6$ **17.** $6x + 4y \geq -8$ **18.** $x + y < 10$

Quiz

Graph an inequality that describes the situation.

1. Jay reads a maximum of 20 pages.   **2.** Mandy hikes more than 7.5 miles.

Write an inequality represented by the graph.

3. 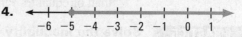   **4.**

Translate the verbal phrase into a compound inequality. Then graph the inequality.

5. All real numbers that are less than -10 *and* greater than or equal to -13.

6. All real numbers that are greater than 6 *or* less than or equal to 0.

Graph the inequality.

7. $y \geq -3x - 4$ **8.** $-2x < y$ **9.** $x - 2y \geq 4$

BENCHMARK 3
(Chapters 5 and 6)

B. Solving Inequalities

If two inequalities have the same solution, then they are equivalent. Solving inequalities is similar, but not identical, to solving equations. Whenever you multiply or divide both sides of the inequality by the same *negative* number, you must reverse the direction of the inequality symbol.

1. Solve an Inequality Using Addition or Subtraction

EXAMPLE   **Solve the inequality. Graph the solution.**

a. $x - 3 < 2$ **b.** $b + 1 \geq -8$

Solution:

Check by substituting a number less than 5 for *x* in the original inequality. Try $x = 4$:

$x - 3 < 2$
$4 - 3 \overset{?}{<} 2$
$1 < 2$ ✔

a.	$x - 3 < 2$	Write original inequality.
	$x - 3 + 3 < 2 + 3$	Add 3 to each side.
	$x < 5$	Simplify.

The solutions are all real numbers less than 5.

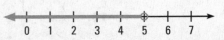

b.	$b + 1 \geq -8$	Write original inequality.
	$b + 1 - 1 \geq -8 - 1$	Subtract 1 from each side.
	$b \geq -9$	Simplify.

The solutions are all real numbers greater than or equal to −9.

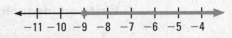

PRACTICE   **Solve the inequality. Graph the solution.**

1. $p + 1.2 > 4.5$ **2.** $m - 2\frac{5}{8} \leq 4\frac{3}{8}$ **3.** $-6 < 27 + k$

4. $\frac{6}{5} + t \geq -5$ **5.** $r - 7.3 < -3.9$ **6.** $14 + m \leq 54$

2. Solve an Inequality Using Multiplication or Division

EXAMPLE   **Solve the inequality. Graph the solution.**

a. $\frac{x}{2} \geq 3$ **b.** $-5x > 15$

Solution:

a.	$\frac{x}{2} \geq 3$	Write original inequality.
	$2 \cdot \frac{x}{2} \geq 3 \cdot 2$	Multiply each side by 2.
	$x \geq 6$	Simplify.

The solutions are all real numbers greater than or equal to 6.

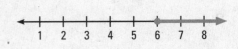

BENCHMARK 3
(Chapters 5 and 6)

Multiplying or dividing each side of an inequality by a negative number and reversing the direction of the inequality produces an *equivalent inequality.*

b. $-5x > 15$ **Write original inequality.**

$$\frac{-5x}{-5} < \frac{15}{-5}$$ **Divide each side by -5 and reverse inequality symbol.**

$x < -3$ **Simplify.**

The solutions are all real numbers less than -3.

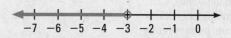

PRACTICE   Solve the inequality. Graph the solution.

7. $16x < 4$ **8.** $-\dfrac{d}{3} \le -9$ **9.** $7c \ge -42$

10. $-6z > 54$ **11.** $\dfrac{w}{5} < 2.3$ **12.** $\dfrac{n}{8} \le -5$

3. Solve a Multi-Step Inequality

EXAMPLE   Solve the inequality. Graph the solution.

a. $2c + 1 \le 6c - 9$ **b.** $-3(m + 2) < -15$

Here's an alternate way to solve this example. Subtract $6c$ and 1 from both sides:

$2c + 1 \le 6c - 9$

$-4c + 1 \le -9$

$-4c \le -10$

$c \ge 2.5$

$c \ge 2.5$ and $2.5 \le c$ are equivalent inequalities.

Solution:

a. $2c + 1 \le 6c - 9$ **Write original inequality.**

$1 \le 4c - 9$ **Subtract $2c$ from both sides.**

$10 \le 4c$ **Add 9 to both sides.**

$2.5 \le c$ **Divide both sides by 4.**

The solutions are all real numbers greater than or equal to 2.5.

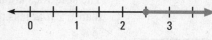

b. $-3(m + 2) < -15$ **Write original inequality.**

$-3m - 6 < -15$ **Distributive property**

$-3m < -9$ **Add 6 to both sides.**

$m > 3$ **Divide both sides by -3 and reverse inequality symbol.**

The solutions are all real numbers greater than 3.

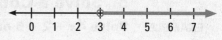

PRACTICE   Solve the inequality. Graph the solution.

13. $3x - 2 > 6 + x$ **14.** $-6t + \dfrac{10}{3} \le \dfrac{2}{3}t$

15. $1.8q + 3.4 < 2.1q - 2.6$ **16.** $\dfrac{1}{2}(3v + 1) \le \dfrac{7}{2}$

17. $-2n - 4 \le 3(n + 2)$ **18.** $-\dfrac{3}{4}(8 + 12a) > 3a$

BENCHMARK 3
B. Solving Inequalities

BENCHMARK 3
(Chapters 5 and 6)

4. Solve a Compound Inequality With *and*

EXAMPLE **Solve $3 \le x - 2 \le 8$. Graph the solution.**

You can solve a compound inequality with *and* by separating the inequality.

Solution:

$3 \le x - 2$	*and*	$x - 2 \le 8$	Write as two separate inequalities.
$3 + 2 \le x - 2 + 2$	*and*	$x - 2 + 2 \le 8 + 2$	Add 2 to each side.
$5 \le x$	*and*	$x \le 10$	Simplify.

The compound inequality can be written $5 \le x \le 10$. The solutions are all real numbers greater than or equal to 5 *and* less than equal to 10.

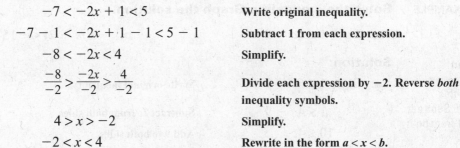

EXAMPLE **Solve $-7 < -2x + 1 < 5$. Graph the solution.**

Solution:

You can also solve a compound inequality with *and* by applying the same operation to each expression in the inequality.

$-7 < -2x + 1 < 5$	Write original inequality.
$-7 - 1 < -2x + 1 - 1 < 5 - 1$	Subtract 1 from each expression.
$-8 < -2x < 4$	Simplify.
$\dfrac{-8}{-2} > \dfrac{-2x}{-2} > \dfrac{4}{-2}$	Divide each expression by -2. Reverse *both* inequality symbols.
$4 > x > -2$	Simplify.
$-2 < x < 4$	Rewrite in the form $a < x < b$.

The solutions are all real numbers greater than -2 *and* less than 4.

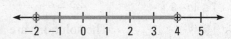

PRACTICE **Solve the inequality. Graph the solution.**

19. $5 < 4a - 7 < 13$ 20. $-4 \le \dfrac{2x}{3} \le 8$ 21. $11 \le -3p + 2 \le 20$

22. $-7 < 6n + 5 \le -1$ 23. $5 < -\dfrac{5w}{3} < 15$ 24. $-7 < -2j - 3 < -1$

5. Solve a Compound Inequality With *or*

EXAMPLE **Solve $4x + 2 < 5$ or $3x - 8 \ge 1$. Graph the solution.**

Solution:

If you get overlapping inequalities, such as $x > 1$ or $x < 3$, the solution is all real numbers.

$4x + 2 < 5$	*or*	$3x - 8 \ge 1$	Write as two separate inequalities.
$4x + 2 - 2 < 5 - 2$	*or*	$3x - 8 + 8 \ge 1 + 8$	Addition or subtraction property of inequality
$4x < 3$	*or*	$3x \ge 9$	Simplify.
$\dfrac{4x}{4} < \dfrac{3}{4}$	*or*	$\dfrac{3x}{3} \ge \dfrac{9}{3}$	Multiplication or division property of inequality
$x < \dfrac{3}{4}$	*or*	$x \ge 3$	Simplify.

The solutions are all real numbers less than $\dfrac{3}{4}$ *or* greater than or equal to 3.

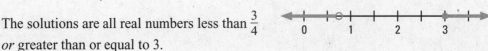

BENCHMARK 3
(Chapters 5 and 6)

PRACTICE **Solve the inequality. Graph the solution.**

25. $-2a + 3 \geq 15$ *or* $1 - a < 4$ **26.** $2n - 5 \geq 3$ *or* $6 - n > 9$

27. $4y + 20 < 0$ *or* $y + 3 > 2$ **28.** $k + 7 \leq 3$ *or* $-2k + 5 < 2$

29. $b - 2 \geq 0$ *or* $b + 4 \leq 5$ **30.** $-\dfrac{j}{5} + 2 < 12$ *or* $j + 40 < -5$

Quiz

Solve the inequality. Graph the solution.

1. $y + 5.3 > 2.9$ **2.** $b - 1\frac{3}{4} \leq 5\frac{1}{4}$ **3.** $-6 < 24 + n$

4. $\dfrac{4}{3} + k \geq -2$ **5.** $d - 1.9 < -5.7$ **6.** $12 + a \leq 63$

7. $15x < 30$ **8.** $-\dfrac{x}{7} \leq -4$ **9.** $8c \geq -32$

10. $-3z > 72$ **11.** $\dfrac{y}{9} < 4.6$ **12.** $\dfrac{b}{12} \leq -40$

13. $3x - 6 > 4 + x$ **14.** $-5s + 1 \leq \frac{1}{2}s$ **15.** $-2.5p + 0.9 < 4.3p - 0.8$

16. $\dfrac{2}{3}(6r + 9) \leq 26$ **17.** $-11m + 1 \geq 2(m - 6)$ **18.** $-\dfrac{2}{5}(5 - 10z) > 3z$

19. $6 < 3g - 3 < 15$ **20.** $-6 \leq \dfrac{2x}{7} \leq 4$ **21.** $11 \leq -4a + 7 \leq 35$

22. $-4 < 6n + 2 \leq 0$ **23.** $8 \leq -\dfrac{4t}{7} < 24$ **24.** $-9 < -j - 19 < -5$

25. $x + 4 > 14$ *or* $x - 2 \leq 4$ **26.** $2x + 6 \leq -10$ *or* $x + 10 > 9$

27. $-2x - 8 < 2$ *or* $x - 2 < 9$ **28.** $\dfrac{1}{2}x - 7 < 6$ *or* $32 - x \leq 0$

29. $x - 3 > 13$ *or* $x + 5 < 9$ **30.** $x - 7 \geq -3$ *or* $-3x + 6 \geq -3$

BENCHMARK 3
B. Solving Inequalities

BENCHMARK 3
(Chapters 5 and 6)

C. Absolute Value Equations and Inequalities

The rules for solving absolute value equations and inequalities are different from those for solving linear equations and inequalities. You must isolate the absolute value expression on one side of the equation or inequality before you can solve it.

1. Solve an Absolute Value Equation

Vocabulary   **Absolute value equation** An equation that includes an absolute value expression.

EXAMPLE   **Solve $|x| = 6$.**

Solution:

$|x| = 6$ means "the distance between x and 0 on a number line is 6 units." Only two numbers are 6 units from 0: 6 and -6.

$|x| = 6$

$x = 6$ or $x = -6$

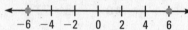

PRACTICE   **Solve the equation.**

1. $|x| = 12$ 2. $|y| = 2.4$ 3. $|b| = \frac{2}{3}$

4. $|m| = 44$ 5. $|r| = 6\frac{5}{8}$ 6. $|p| = 0.9$

2. Solve an Absolute Value Equation in Multiple Steps

EXAMPLE   **Solve $4|3x - 1| - 6 = 10$.**

Solution:

Step 1: Rewrite the equation in the form $|ax + b| = c$.

$4|3x - 1| - 6 = 10$	**Write original equation.**
$4|3x - 1| = 16$	**Add 6 to each side.**
$|3x - 1| = 4$	**Divide each side by 4.**

You cannot add 1 to both sides of $|3x - 1| = 4$.

Step 2: Solve the absolute value equation.

$|3x - 1| = 4$	**Write absolute value equation.**
$3x - 1 = 4$ *or* $3x - 1 = -4$	**Rewrite as two equations.**
$3x = 5$ *or* $3x = -3$	**Add 1 to each side.**
$x = \frac{5}{3}$ *or* $x = -1$	**Divide each side by 3.**

$|3x - 1| = 4$ and $|3x| = 5$ are NOT equivalent statements.

PRACTICE   **Solve the equation.**

7. $5|x + 3| + 4 = 19$ 8. $3|2c - 4| + 5 = 17$ 9. $\frac{1}{2}|4p - 7| - 2 = 8$

10. $-|3t - 8| - 5 = -9$ 11. $3|-2z + 5| - 2 = 7$ 12. $\frac{3}{2}\left|\frac{6}{5}a - 3\right| - 2 = 1$

BENCHMARK 3
(Chapters 5 and 6)

3. Solve an Absolute Value Inequality

EXAMPLE   Solve the inequality. Graph the solution.

a. $|x + 11| \geq 4$ **b.** $|2x - 6| + 1 < 9$

Solution:

The solution of an absolute value inequality with $<$ or $\leq$ is values *between* a number and its opposite.

The solution of an absolute value inequality with $>$ or $\geq$ is values *beyond* a number and its opposite.

a. $|x + 11| \geq 4$ Write original inequality.

$x + 11 \leq -4 \quad or \quad x + 11 \geq 4$ The inequality symbol is $\geq$. Rewrite as compound inequality in form $ax + b \leq -c$ or $ax + b \geq c$.

$x \leq -15 \quad or \qquad x \geq -7$ Subtract 11 from each side.

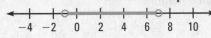
$-16 \; -14 \; -12 \; -10 \; -8 \; -6 \; -4 \; -2$

b. $|2x - 6| + 1 < 9$ Write original inequality.

$|2x - 6| < 8$ Subtract 1 from each side.

$-8 < 2x - 6 < 8$ The inequality symbol is $<$. Rewrite as compound inequality in form $-c < ax + b < c$.

$-2 < 2x < 14$ Add 6 to each expression.

$-1 < x < 7$ Divide each expression by 2.

$-4 \; -2 \quad 0 \quad 2 \quad 4 \quad 6 \quad 8 \quad 10$

PRACTICE   Solve the equation. Graph the solution.

13. $|x - 7| < 2$ **14.** $5|2a - 4| \geq 15$ **15.** $|n + 5| - 8 > 3$

16. $-6\left|3t + \dfrac{5}{6}\right| - 4 \leq -5$ **17.** $\dfrac{2}{3}|4q + 1| + 3 < 9$ **18.** $6|-5f + 2| + 4 \leq 16$

Quiz

Solve the equation.

1. $|a| = 14$ **2.** $|c| = 9.7$ **3.** $|x| = \dfrac{4}{9}$

4. $|n| = 38$ **5.** $|s| = 1\dfrac{6}{7}$ **6.** $|q| = 0.3$

7. $2|x + 4| + 1 = 7$ **8.** $6|3u - 2| + 5 = 41$ **9.** $\dfrac{1}{4}|2q - 3| - 6 = 4$

10. $-|8t + 7| - 2 = -5$ **11.** $4|-4y + 3| - 9 = 15$ **12.** $\dfrac{3}{4}\left|\dfrac{2}{5}r - 6\right| - 23 = 1$

Solve the equation. Graph the solution.

13. $|x - 35| < 68$ **14.** $4|7a - 2| \geq 20$ **15.** $|t + 3| - 7 > 53$

16. $-4|6t + 4.5| - 3 \leq -5.4$ **17.** $\dfrac{1}{6}|3b + 2| + 4 < 8$ **18.** $5|-2k + 1| + 3 \leq 18$

BENCHMARK 3
(Chapters 5 and 6)

D. Solving Linear Systems by Graphing

A linear system can have zero, one, or infinitely many solutions. One way to find this solution is to graph each equation in the system. The point where the lines intersect is the solution to the system. If the graph of the equations are parallel lines, then no point of intersection exists, and the system has no solution. If each equation represents the same line, the system has infinitely many solutions.

1. Checking Solutions to Linear Systems

Vocabulary

System of linear equations Two or more linear equations in the same variables; also called a *linear system*.

EXAMPLE

Tell whether the ordered pair is a solution of the linear system.

For a linear system with one solution, the solution is an ordered pair that satisfies each equation in the system.

a. $(2, 1)$;

$2x - y = 3$ **Equation 1**
$-x + 3y = 1$ **Equation 2**

b. $(0, 5)$;

$4x - 2y = -10$ **Equation 1**
$3x + y = 15$ **Equation 2**

Solution:

a. Substitute 2 for x and 1 for y in each equation.

$2x - y = 3$	$-x + 3y = 1$
$2(2) - (1) \stackrel{?}{=} 3$	$-2 + 3(1) \stackrel{?}{=} 1$
$4 - 1 \stackrel{?}{=} 3$	$-2 + 3 \stackrel{?}{=} 1$
$3 = 3$ ✔	$1 = 1$ ✔

The ordered pair $(2, 1)$ is a solution of each equation, so it is the solution of the system.

b. Substitute 0 for x and 5 for y in each equation.

$4x - 2y = -10$	$3x + y = 15$
$4(0) - 2(5) \stackrel{?}{=} -10$	$3(0) + 5 \stackrel{?}{=} 15$
$0 - 10 \stackrel{?}{=} -10$	$0 + 5 \stackrel{?}{=} 15$
$-10 = -10$ ✔	$5 = 15$ ✗

The ordered pair $(0, 5)$ is NOT the solution of $3x + y = 15$, so it is NOT the solution of the system.

PRACTICE **Tell whether the ordered pair is a solution of the linear system.**

1. $(4, -2)$;
$3x + 3y = 6$
$-2x + 4y = -16$

2. $(-3, 3)$;
$x + 2y = 3$
$-2x - 3y = -3$

3. $(-1, 0)$;
$6x + 4y = -6$
$5x - 2y = 2$

4. $(3, 6)$;
$2x - 3y = 12$
$-x + 5y = 27$

5. $(2, -8)$;
$10x + 5y = -20$
$-3x - y = -2$

6. $(1, 5)$;
$4x - 2y = -6$
$-3x + 4y = 17$

BENCHMARK 3
D. Solving Systems

BENCHMARK 3
(Chapters 5 and 6)

2. Graphing Linear Systems

EXAMPLE **Use the graph to solve the system. Then check your solution algebraically.**

$x - y = -3$ **Equation 1**
$x + y = 1$ **Equation 2**

Solution:

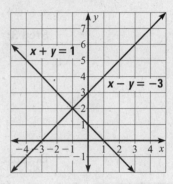

The lines seem to intersect at $(-1, 2)$. Check by substituting -1 for x and 2 for y in each equation.

$$
\begin{array}{c|c}
x - y = -3 & x + y = 1 \\
-1 - 2 \stackrel{?}{=} -3 & -1 + 2 \stackrel{?}{=} 1 \\
-3 = -3 \ \checkmark & 1 = 1 \ \checkmark
\end{array}
$$

The ordered pair $(-1, 2)$ is the solution of each equation. So, $(-1, 2)$ is the solution of the system.

PRACTICE **Use the graph to solve the system. Then check your solution algebraically.**

7.

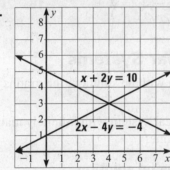

8.

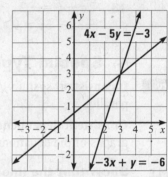

9.

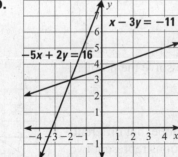

3. Graph-and-Check Method

Vocabulary **Consistent independent system** A linear system with exactly one solution.

EXAMPLE **Solve the linear system:**

$3x - y = 2$ **Equation 1**
$x + 2y = 10$ **Equation 2**

BENCHMARK 3
(Chapters 5 and 6)

Solution:

Step 1: Graph both equations.

Step 2: Estimate the point of intersection.
The two lines appear to intersect at (2, 4).

Step 3: Check whether (2, 4) is a solution by substituting 2 for x and 4 for y in each of the original equations.

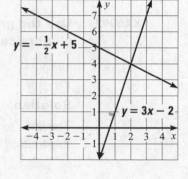

$y = -\frac{1}{2}x + 5$

$y = 3x - 2$

Equation 1	Equation 2
$3x - y = 2$	$x + 2y = 10$
$3(2) - 4 \stackrel{?}{=} 2$	$2 + 2(4) \stackrel{?}{=} 10$
$2 = 2$ ✔	$10 = 10$ ✔

Because (2, 4) is a solution of each equation, it is a solution of the linear system.

PRACTICE

Solve the linear system by graphing. Check your solution.

10. $3x + y = 5$
$5x - 2y = 12$

11. $4x - 2y = -10$
$2x + y = 1$

12. $-2x + y = -9$
$x - 3y = 12$

13. $2x - y = -2$
$-3x + 3y = 9$

14. $6x - 4y = 4$
$x - y = 0$

15. $2x + 2y = 6$
$-x + 2y = -9$

4. Special Types of Linear Systems

Vocabulary

Inconsistent system A linear system with no solution; the graphs of the equations are parallel.

Consistent dependent system A linear system with infinitely many solutions; the graphs of the equations are the same line.

EXAMPLE

Show that the linear system has no solution.

$2x - 3y = -3$ **Equation 1**
$2x - 3y = 15$ **Equation 2**

Solution:

You can use either of two methods to solve the problem.

Method 1: Graphing

Lines that do not intersect are said to be *inconsistent*. So, a linear system with no solutions is an inconsistent system.

Graph the linear system.

The lines have the same slope, but different y-intercepts. So, the equations represent two parallel lines, which do not intersect. The system has no solution.

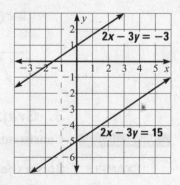

$2x - 3y = -3$

$2x - 3y = 15$

BENCHMARK 3
D. Solving Systems

BENCHMARK 3
(Chapters 5 and 6)

Method 2: Elimination

Subtract the equations.

$$2x - 3y = -3$$
$$- (2x - 3y = 15)$$

$\longrightarrow$

$$2x - 3y = -3$$
$$-2x + 3y = -15$$
$$\overline{\hspace{2em} 0 = -18 \ \text{✗}} \longleftarrow \text{This is a false statement.}$$

Subtracting the equations leads to a false statement, so the system has no solution.

EXAMPLE **Show that the linear system has infinitely many solutions.**

$y = \dfrac{3}{4}x - 2$ **Equation 1**

$3x - 4y = 8$ **Equation 2**

Solution:

You can use either of two methods to solve the problem.

Method 1: Graphing

Graph the linear system.

Both equations represent the same line. So, all points on the line are solutions. The system has infinitely many solutions.

Lines that intersect are said to be *consistent,* and equations that are equivalent are said to be *dependent.* So, a linear system in which all the equations represent the same line is a consistent, dependent system.

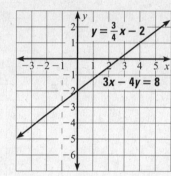

Method 2: Substitution

Substitute $\dfrac{3}{4}x - 2$ for y in Equation 2 and solve for x.

$$3x - 4y = 8 \qquad\qquad \text{Write Equation 2.}$$
$$3x - 4\left(\dfrac{3}{4}x - 2\right) = 8 \qquad \text{Substitute } \dfrac{3}{4}x - 2 \text{ for } y.$$
$$3x - 3x + 8 = 8 \qquad\qquad \text{Simplify.}$$
$$8 = 8 \qquad\qquad\qquad \text{Simplify.}$$

Substitution leads to a statement that is always true. The system has infinitely many solutions.

PRACTICE **Tell whether the linear system has *no solution* or *infinitely many solutions.* Explain.**

16. $x - 4y = -20$
$x - 4y = 8$

17. $y = -\dfrac{3}{4}x - 6$
$3x + 4y = -24$

18. $3x - 2y = -8$
$-3x + 2y = -6$

19. $3x + \dfrac{1}{3}y = 1$
$9x + y = -6$

20. $y = -5x + 3$
$10x + 2y = 6$

21. $14y - 6x = -28$
$3x - 7y = 14$

BENCHMARK 3
D. Solving Systems

BENCHMARK 3
(Chapters 5 and 6)

Quiz

Tell whether the ordered pair is a solution of the linear system.

1. $(-3, 2)$;
$x - 2y = -7$
$3x - 2y = -13$

2. $(-7, -5)$;
$x + y = -12$
$2x - 4y = -34$

3. $(9, -10)$;
$2x + y = 8$
$-3x + 4y = -67$

Use the graph to solve the system. Then check your solution algebraically.

4.
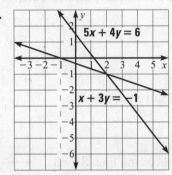

5.
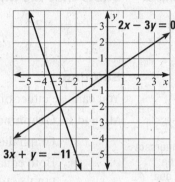

6.
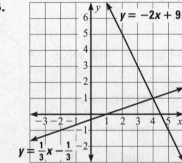

Solve the linear system. If the system has one solution, check the solution. If the system has no solution or infinitely many solutions, explain.

7. $x + 4y = 2$
$3x - 5y = 6$

8. $3x + y = -4$
$y = -3x + 1$

9. $8x - 6y = -2$
$x + 3y = -4$

10. $x - 4y = -3$
$-2x + 6y = 2$

11. $2x + y = 1$
$5x + 3y = 0$

12. $2y = -x + 8$
$2x + 4y = 16$

BENCHMARK 3
D. Solving Systems

Benchmark 3
(Chapters 5 and 6)

E. Solving Linear Systems Using Algebra

A **system of linear equations** is two or more linear equations with the same variables. The **solution of a system of linear equations** is an ordered pair that satisfies each equation in the system. The following examples describe methods which can be used to find the solution of a system of two linear equations.

1. Solve a Linear System by Substitution

Vocabulary   **Substitution** Replacing a variable in an equation by an expression or a value.

EXAMPLE   **Solve the linear system:**

$2x - 3 = y$ **Equation 1**
$3x - 2y = 4$ **Equation 2**

Solution:

Step 1: Solve for a variable in one of the equations.

$$y = 2x - 3$$ **Equation 1 is already solved for *y*.**

Step 2: Substitute the expressions from Step 1 into the other equation and solve.

Don't stop after solving for one variable. The system is not solved until a solution is found for both variables.

$3x - 2y = 4$ **Write Equation 2.**
$3x - 2(2x - 3) = 4$ **Substitute $2x - 3$ for *y* into Equation 2.**
$3x - 4x + 6 = 4$ **Simplify.**
$-x = -2$ **Combine like terms.**
$x = 2$ **Multiply each side by -1.**

Step 3: Use the value found in Step 2 to find the value of the other variable.

$y = 2x - 3 = 2(2) - 3 = 1$ **Substitute $x = 2$ into Equation 1.**

The solution is $(2, 1)$.

PRACTICE   **Use the substitution method to solve the linear system.**

1. $y = 2x + 5$
$3x + y = 10$

2. $x = y + 3$
$x + 2y = -6$

3. $2x + 4y = 0$
$3x + 7 = y$

4. $x + 2y = -5$
$4x - 3y = 2$

5. $3x - 2y = 4$
$x + 3y = 5$

6. $3x + y = -2$
$x + 3y = 2$

2. Solve a Linear System by Adding or Subtracting

Vocabulary   **Elimination** Performing operations on and combining two or more equations in a system in such a way that one of the variables is no longer present.

BENCHMARK 3
(Chapters 5 and 6)

EXAMPLE   **Solve the linear system:**

$2x + 3y = 9$ **Equation 1**

$2y - 2x = -4$ **Equation 2**

Check solutions by substituting them into the original equations to see if the resulting statements are true.

Solution:

Step 1: Add the equations to eliminate one variable and solve.

$$
\begin{aligned}
2x + 3y &= 9 \\
+\ -2x + 2y &= -4 \\
\hline
5y &= 5 \\
y &= 1
\end{aligned}
$$

Add Equation 1 and Equation 2.

Solve for y.

Step 2: Use the value found in Step 1 to find the value of the other variable.

$2x + 3y = 9$ **Write Equation 1.**

$2x + 3(1) = 9$ **Substitute $y = 1$ into Equation 1.**

$2x = 6$ **Simplify.**

$x = 3$ **Divide each side by 2.**

The solution is (3, 1).

EXAMPLE   **Solve the linear system:**

$4x + 3y = 3$ **Equation 1**

$9 = 2x + 3y$ **Equation 2**

Solution:

Step 1: Subtract the equations to eliminate one variable and solve.

When subtracting equations, make sure each term of the second equation is subtracted from each like term in the first equation.

$$
\begin{aligned}
4x + 3y &= 3 \\
-\ 2x + 3y &= 9 \\
\hline
2x &= -6 \\
x &= -3
\end{aligned}
$$

Subtract Equation 1 and Equation 2.

Solve for x.

Step 2: Use the value found in Step 1 to find the value of the other variable.

$4x + 3y = 3$ **Write Equation 1.**

$4(-3) + 3y = 3$ **Substitute $x = -3$ into Equation 1.**

$3y = 15$ **Simplify.**

$y = 5$ **Divide each side by 3.**

The solution is (−3, 5).

BENCHMARK 3
E. Solving Systems using Algebra

Benchmark 3
(Chapters 5 and 6)

PRACTICE Use the method of adding or subtracting equations to solve the linear system.

7. $2x = 3y$
$x + 3y = 9$

8. $4x + 3y = 8$
$-y + 4x = -8$

9. $5x - 2y = 20$
$3x + 4 = -2y$

10. $3y - 4x = 3$
$-x + 3y = -15$

11. $3x - 7 = 5y$
$3x + 4y = -11$

12. $-2x = y - 3$
$7x + y = 3$

3. Solve a Linear System by Multiplying First

EXAMPLE Solve the linear system:

$-2x + 4y = 2$ **Equation 1**
$-5x + 6y = -3$ **Equation 2**

Solution:

Step 1: Modify the original system by multiplying both equations by a constant. Use the least common multiple of the coefficients for one of the variables to determine the constants.

$-2x + 4y = 2$ $(\times 3)$ $\rightarrow$ $-6x + 12y = 6$ **The least common**
$-5x + 6y = -3$ $(\times -2)$ $\rightarrow$ $10x - 12y = 6$ **multiple of 4 and 6 is 12, so multiply Equation 1 by 3 to get 12y and Equation 2 by −2 to get −12y.**

Step 2: Add the modified equations from Step 1 and solve.

$$\begin{array}{r} -6x + 12y = 6 \\ +\ 10x - 12y = 6 \\ \hline 4x = 12 \\ x = 3 \end{array}$$

     Add the modified equations.

     Solve for x.

Step 3: Use the value found in Step 2 to find the value of the other variable.

$-2x + 4y = 2$ **Write Equation 1.**

$-2(3) + 4y = 2$ **Substitute x = 3 into Equation 1.**

$4y = 8$ **Simplify.**

$y = 2$ **Divide each side by 4.**

The solution is (3, 2).

PRACTICE Multiply one or both equations by constants to solve the linear system.

13. $2x + 12 = 2y$
$3x + y = -10$

14. $5x + 2y = 14$
$2x - 3y = -2$

15. $5y - 4x = -1$
$6x - 7y = 3$

16. $3y - 2x = -10$
$4x + 7y = -6$

17. $6y - 5x = 8$
$7x - 8y = -12$

18. $3x - 2y = -3$
$9x - 4y = 3$

E. Solving Systems using Algebra

BENCHMARK 3

BENCHMARK 3
(Chapters 5 and 6)

Quiz

Use the substitution method to find the solution to the set of equations.

1. $x + 3y = 10$
$2x - y = 6$

2. $5x = y - 1$
$3x + 9 = 2y$

3. $5y - 2x = -4$
$x - 3y = 3$

Use the elimination method to find the solution to the set of equations.

4. $4x = 3y - 6$
$x + 3y = -9$

5. $2x + 5y = 3$
$2x + 7y = 5$

6. $4y - 5x = 3$
$3x = 4y - 5$

7. $2x - 3y = 0$
$3x - 4y = 1$

8. $4y - 3x = -1$
$5x - 2y = -3$

9. $3x + 2y = 2$
$6x + 5y = 8$

For each linear system, name the method which is most appropriate for solving the system: substitution, adding equations, subtracting equations, or multiplying first. Then solve the system.

10. $2y = 5x + 3$
$-3x + 2y = 5$

11. $4x = 3y - 4$
$3x - y = 2$

12. $5x + 6y = -4$
$4x + 3y = -5$

13. You have 50 tickets to ride the Ferris wheel and the roller coaster. If you ride 12 times total, using 3 tickets for each Ferris wheel ride and 5 tickets for each roller coaster ride, how many times did you go on each ride?

BENCHMARK 3
E. Solving Systems using Algebra

Benchmark 3
(Chapters 5 and 6)

F. Solving Systems of Linear Inequalities

One way to solve a system of inequalities is to graph each inequality. The graph of the system is the intersection of these graphs.

1. Graphing Systems of Two Linear Inequalities

Vocabulary

System of linear inequalities Two or more linear inequalities in the same variables; also called a *system of inequalities*.

EXAMPLE

Recall that inequalities with < or > symbols are graphed with dashed lines, while inequalities with ≤ or ≥ symbols are graphed with solid lines.

Graph the system of inequalities.

$y \leq x + 3$ **Inequality 1**
$y > -2x - 1$ **Inequality 2**

Solution:

Graph both inequalities in the same coordinate plane. The graph of the system is the intersection of the two half-planes, which is shown as the darkest gray.

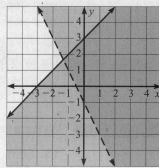

PRACTICE

Graph the system of inequalities.

1. $y > 4x + 1$
$y < -x - 2$

2. $y \geq x - 4$
$y \leq -3x + 4$

3. $x - 2y < -4$
$y \geq -2$

4. $y \leq 2x - 2$
$2x + 3y < 1$

5. $x > -3$
$x \geq -1$

6. $y > 1$
$x \leq 4$

2. Graphing Systems of Three Linear Inequalities

EXAMPLE

Graph the system of inequalities.

$y \leq -3x + 2$ **Inequality 1**
$x > -1$ **Inequality 2**
$x \leq 2$ **Inequality 3**

Solution:

Graph all three inequalities in the same coordinate plane. The graph of the system is the shaded region shown.

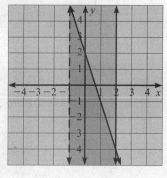

PRACTICE

Choose a point in the shaded region and substitute it in each inequality. The solution checks if each substitution results in a true statement.

Graph the system of inequalities.

7. $y \geq -2x - 1$
$y \geq 2x - 1$
$y > 4$

8. $y \geq x$
$x < 4$
$y > -1$

9. $y < x + 4$
$4x + y < 4$
$y \geq -4$

10. $y < 2$
$y > 2x$
$y \leq -x + 3$

11. $2x + 3y \leq -2$
$y \geq -2x - 8$
$y > 3x + 6$

12. $x < -3$
$x < 0$
$y \geq 0$

BENCHMARK 3
F. Systems of Linear Inequalities

BENCHMARK 3
(Chapters 5 and 6)

3. Write a System of Linear Inequalities

EXAMPLE **Write a system of inequalities for the shaded region.**

Solution:

Find the equation of the lines from the slope and y-intercept, from two points, or from a point and the slope.

Inequality 1 One boundary line for the shaded region is $y = 5$. Because the shaded region is *below* the *solid* line, the inequality is $y \le 5$.

Inequality 2 Another boundary line for the shaded region has a slope of 1 and a y-intercept of 3. So, its equation is $y = x + 3$. Because the shaded region is *below* the *dashed* line, the inequality is $y < x + 3$.

The system of inequalities for the shaded region is:

$$y \le 5 \qquad \text{Inequality 1}$$
$$y < x + 3 \qquad \text{Inequality 2}$$

PRACTICE **Write a system of inequalities for the shaded region.**

13.

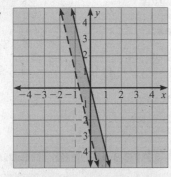

14.

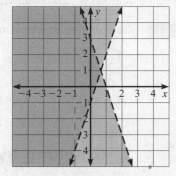

15.

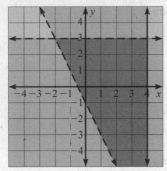

BENCHMARK 3
F. Systems of Linear Inequalities

Benchmark 3
(Chapters 5 and 6)

Quiz

Graph the system of inequalities.

1. $x \leq -5$
$y \geq -1$

2. $x + 2y > -1$
$y > -3$

3. $x + y \geq -2$
$x + y > -6$
$4x + y < -4$

4. $y \geq -2$
$y \leq 1$
$x \geq 0$

5. $x > 1$
$x > 2$
$x > 3$

6. $y < -5x + 3$
$y \leq -4x - 2$
$4x - 3y < -3$

Write a system of inequalities for the shaded region.

7.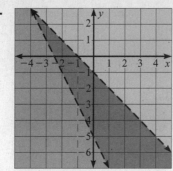

8.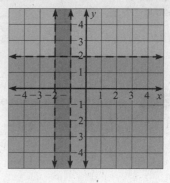

9.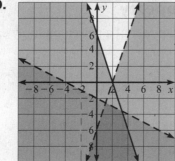

BENCHMARK 4
(Chapters 7 and 8)

A. Properties of Exponents

A **power** represents repeated multiplication. The following examples illustrate several properties that you can use to simplify expressions with powers.

1. Product of Powers Property

Vocabulary   **Product of Powers Property** To multiply powers having the same base, add the exponents.

EXAMPLE   **Simplify the expression.**

If a is a real number and m and n are positive integers, $a^m \cdot a^n = a^{m+n}$.

a. $4^2 \cdot 4^8$ b. $3 \cdot 3^7 \cdot 3^6$ c. $(-12)(-12)^4$ d. $x^2 \cdot x^{10} \cdot x^5$

Solution:

a. $4^2 \cdot 4^8$ b. $3 \cdot 3^7 \cdot 3^6$ c. $(-12)(-12)^4$ d. $x^2 \cdot x^{10} \cdot x^5$
$= 4^{2+8}$ $= 3^1 \cdot 3^7 \cdot 3^6$ $= (-12)^1 \cdot (-12)^4$ $= x^{2+10+5}$
$= 4^{10}$ $= 3^{1+7+6}$ $= (-12)^{1+4}$ $= x^{17}$
                          $= 3^{14}$ $= (-12)^5$

PRACTICE   **Simplify the expression.**

1. $8^7 \cdot 8^2$ 2. $5^3 \cdot 5 \cdot 5^9$ 3. $(-6)^7(-6)^4(-6)$

4. $d^{10} \cdot d^7$ 5. $r^5 \cdot r^7 \cdot r^8$ 6. $k^2 \cdot k^3 \cdot k$

2. Power of a Power Property

Vocabulary   **Power of a Power Property** To find a power of a power, multiply exponents.

EXAMPLE   **Simplify the expression.**

If a is a real number and m and n are positive integers, $(a^m)^n = a^{mn}$.

a. $(3^2)^4$ b. $[(-4)^9]^2$ c. $(x^3)^3$ d. $[(y-3)^5]^4$

Solution:

a. $(3^2)^4 = 3^{2 \cdot 4}$ b. $[(-4)^9]^2$ c. $(x^3)^3 = x^{3 \cdot 3}$ d. $[(y-3)^5]^4$
$= 3^8$ $= (-4)^{9 \cdot 2}$ $= x^9$ $= (y-3)^{5 \cdot 4}$
                                $= (-4)^{18}$ $= (y-3)^{20}$

PRACTICE   **Simplify the expression.**

7. $(10^3)^6$ 8. $[(-6)^2]^8$ 9. $(t^5)^3$

10. $(b^4)^4$ 11. $[(p+5)^7]^2$ 12. $[(h-1)^9]^5$

Benchmark 4
(Chapters 7 and 8)

3. Power of a Product Property

Vocabulary

Power of a Product Property To find a power of a product, find the power of each factor and multiply.

EXAMPLE

Evaluate the numerical power when simplifying powers with both numerical and variable bases.

Simplify the expression.

a. $(9 \cdot 7)^3$ **b.** $(5xy)^2$ **c.** $(-3z)^4$ **d.** $-(3z)^4$

Solution:

a. $(9 \cdot 7)^3$
$= 9^3 \cdot 7^3$

b. $(5xy)^2$
$= (5 \cdot x \cdot y)^2$
$= 5^2 \cdot x^2 \cdot y^2$
$= 25x^2y^2$

c. $(-3z)^4$
$= (-3 \cdot z)^4$
$= (-3)^4 \cdot z^4$
$= 81z^4$

d. $-(3z)^4$
$= -(3 \cdot z)^4$
$= -(3^4 \cdot z^4)$
$= -81z^4$

PRACTICE

If a and b are real numbers and m is a positive integer, $(ab)^m = a^m b^m$.

Simplify the expression.

13. $(5 \cdot 4)^6$ **14.** $(3gh)^3$ **15.** $(6cd)^2$

16. $(-2p)^4$ **17.** $-(5t)^3$ **18.** $-(-8a)^2$

4. Quotient of Powers Property

Vocabulary

Quotient of Powers Property To divide powers having the same base, subtract exponents.

EXAMPLE

If a is a nonzero real number and m and n are positive integers such that $m > n$, $\frac{a^m}{a^n} = a^{m-n}, a \neq 0$.

Simplify the expression.

a. $\frac{9^7}{9^3}$ **b.** $\frac{(-6)^{10}}{(-6)^8}$ **c.** $\frac{3^9 \cdot 3^5}{3^4}$ **d.** $\frac{1}{x^5} \cdot x^{12}$

Solution:

a. $\frac{9^7}{9^3}$
$= 9^{7-3}$
$= 9^4$

b. $\frac{(-6)^{10}}{(-6)^8}$
$= (-6)^{10-8}$
$= (-6)^2$

c. $\frac{3^9 \cdot 3^5}{3^4} = \frac{3^{14}}{3^4}$
$= 3^{14-4}$
$= 3^{10}$

d. $\frac{1}{x^5} \cdot x^{12} = \frac{x^{12}}{x^5}$
$= x^{12-5}$
$= x^7$

PRACTICE

Simplify the expression.

19. $\frac{18^{23}}{18^{17}}$ **20.** $\frac{2^{35}}{2^3}$ **21.** $\frac{(-25)^3}{(-25)}$

22. $\frac{4^6 \cdot 4^9}{4^3}$ **23.** $\frac{1}{n^8} \cdot n^{12}$ **24.** $w^6 \cdot \frac{1}{w^4}$

BENCHMARK 4
A. Properties of Exponents

BENCHMARK 4
(Chapters 7 and 8)

5. Power of a Quotient Property

Vocabulary   **Power of a Quotient Property** To find a power of a quotient, find the power of the numerator and the power of the denominator and divide.

EXAMPLE   **Simplify the expression.**

If a and b are real numbers and m is a positive integer, $\left(\dfrac{a}{b}\right)^m = \dfrac{a^m}{b^m}$, $b \neq 0$.

a. $\left(\dfrac{a}{b}\right)^7$ **b.** $\left(-\dfrac{2}{x}\right)^3$

Solution:

a. $\left(\dfrac{a}{b}\right)^7 = \dfrac{a^7}{b^7}$

b. $\left(-\dfrac{2}{x}\right)^3 = \left(\dfrac{-2}{x}\right)^3 = \dfrac{(-2)^3}{x^3} = -\dfrac{8}{x^3}$

PRACTICE   **Simplify the expression.**

25. $\left(\dfrac{2}{5}\right)^3$ **26.** $\left(-\dfrac{5}{8}\right)^2$ **27.** $\left(\dfrac{1}{p}\right)^8$

28. $\left(\dfrac{r}{s}\right)^6$ **29.** $\left(-\dfrac{u}{v}\right)^9$ **30.** $\left(-\dfrac{2}{b}\right)^5$

6. Zero and Negative Exponents

Vocabulary   **Zero power** a to the zero power is 1.
Negative exponents a^{-n} is the reciprocal of a^n, a^n is the reciprocal of a^{-n}.

EXAMPLE   **Simplify the expression.**

a. 5^{-3} **b.** $(-12)^0$ **c.** $\left(\dfrac{1}{2}\right)^{-5}$ **d.** 0^{-4}

If a is a real number ($a \neq 0$) and n is an integer, $a^0 = 1$, $a^{-n} = \dfrac{1}{a^n}$, and $a^n = \dfrac{1}{a^{-n}}$.

Solution:

a. $5^{-3} = \dfrac{1}{5^3}$ **b.** $(-12)^0 = 1$ **c.** $\left(\dfrac{1}{2}\right)^{-5} = \dfrac{1}{\left(\dfrac{1}{2}\right)^5}$ **d.** $0^{-4} = \dfrac{1}{0^4}$

$= \dfrac{1}{125}$ $= \dfrac{1}{\dfrac{1}{32}}$ **Division by 0 is undefined.**

$= 32$

PRACTICE   **Simplify the expression.**

31. 11^{-2} **32.** $\left(\dfrac{5}{8}\right)^0$ **33.** $\left(\dfrac{1}{4}\right)^{-3}$

34. $(-3)^{-4}$ **35.** $\dfrac{1}{6^{-2}}$ **36.** $(-25)^0$

BENCHMARK 4
A. Properties of Exponents

Name _____   Date _____

Benchmark 4
(Chapters 7 and 8)

Quiz

Simplify the expression.

1. $7^4 \cdot 7 \cdot 7^5$

2. $(-8)^3(-8)^9(-8)$

3. $y^{12} \cdot y^8 \cdot y^9$

4. $(6^5)^3$

5. $[(-4)^3]^7$

6. $(s^6)^2$

7. $[(a+11)^8]^4$

8. $(8 \cdot 2)^{13}$

9. $(-5jk)^7$

10. $\dfrac{3^9 \cdot 3^6}{3^2}$

11. $\dfrac{1}{v^8} \cdot v^{17}$

12. $\left(-\dfrac{3}{4}\right)^3$

13. $\left(\dfrac{4}{h}\right)^2$

14. $\left(-\dfrac{p}{q}\right)^{15}$

15. $\left(\dfrac{2}{7}\right)^0$

16. $(-2)^{-5}$

17. $\dfrac{1}{7^{-2}}$

18. $(-13)^0$

BENCHMARK 4
(Chapters 7 and 8)

B. Exponential Functions

A function in the form $y = ab^x$, where $a \neq 0$, $b > 0$, and $b \neq 1$, is an **exponential function.** If a is greater than 0 and b is greater than 1, the function represents exponential growth. If a is greater than 0 and b is between 0 and 1, the function represents exponential decay. The graph of an exponential function is a curved line.

1. Graph an Exponential Growth Function

Vocabulary **Exponential growth** Each time the value of x increases by 1, the value of y is multiplied by a constant amount b, where $b > 1$.

EXAMPLE **Graph the function $y = 3^x$. Identify its domain and range.**

Solution:

Step 1: Choose several values for x and find the values of y.
The domain is all real numbers.

x	-2	-1	0	1	2
y	$\frac{1}{9}$	$\frac{1}{3}$	1	3	9

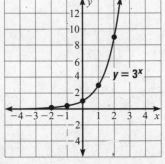

Step 2: Plot the points.

Step 3: Draw a smooth curve through the points.
The range is all positive real numbers.

PRACTICE **Graph the function. Identify its domain and range.**

1. $y = 5^x$

2. $y = 6^x$

3. $y = (3.1)^x$

4. $y = (2.7)^x$

5. $y = \left(\frac{3}{2}\right)^x$

6. $y = \left(\frac{6}{5}\right)^x$

2. Use an Exponential Growth Model

Vocabulary **Exponential growth model** The equation $y = a(1 + r)^t$ is a model of exponential growth where a is the initial value, r is the growth rate, $1 + r$ is the growth factor, and t is the time period.

EXAMPLE **In 1999, Tom's Cafe paid $12,500 for electricity. The cafe's electricity costs since then have increased at a rate of 2.4% per year.**

a. Write a function that models the cafe's electricity costs over time.

b. How much did the cafe pay for electricity in 2004? Round your answer to the nearest whole dollar.

Benchmark 4
(Chapters 7 and 8)

Solution:

a. Let E be the cost of electricity, and let t be the time (in years) since 1999. The initial value a is \$12,500, and the growth rate r is 0.024.

$E = a(1 + r)^t$	**Write exponential growth model.**
$\quad = 12,500(1 + 0.024)^t$	**Substitute 12,500 for a and 0.024 for r.**
$\quad = 12,500(1.024)^t$	**Simplify.**

b. 2004 is 5 years after 1999. Substitute 5 for t.

$E = 12,500(1.024)^5$	**Substitute 5 for t.**
$\quad \approx 14,074$	**Use a calculator.**

In 2004, Tom's Cafe paid about \$14,074 for electricity.

PRACTICE   **Solve.**

7. The population of Hapsville was 245,000 in 1995. The population grows exponentially at 1.8% per year.

   a. Write a function that models the population of Hapsville over time.

   b. What was the population of Hapsville in 2005? Round your answer to the nearest whole number.

8. A newly-discovered plant grows in a lab at a rate of 4.3% per month. On March 1, the plant was 3.75 inches tall.

   a. Write a function that models the plant's height over time.

   b. How tall is the plant by December 1? Round your answer to the nearest hundredth of an inch.

3. Graph an Exponential Decay Function

Vocabulary   **Exponential decay** Each time the value of x increases by 1, the value of y is multiplied by a constant amount b, where $0 < b < 1$.

EXAMPLE   **Graph the function $y = (0.625)^x$. Identify its domain and range.**

Solution:

Step 1: Choose several values for x and find the values of y. The domain is all real numbers.

x	-3	-2	-1	0	1
y	4.096	2.56	1.6	1	0.625

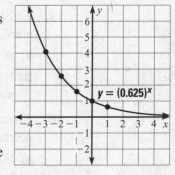

Step 2: Plot the points.

Step 3: Draw a smooth curve through the points. The range is all positive real numbers.

BENCHMARK 4
B. Exponential Functions

BENCHMARK 4
(Chapters 7 and 8)

PRACTICE **Graph the function. Identify its domain and range.**

9. $y = \left(\dfrac{2}{5}\right)^x$ 10. $y = (0.125)^x$ 11. $y = \left(\dfrac{5}{6}\right)^x$

12. $y = (0.9)^x$ 13. $y = \left(\dfrac{10}{11}\right)^x$ 14. $y = (0.3)^x$

4. Use an Exponential Decay Model

Vocabulary **Exponential decay model** The equation $y = a(1 - r)^t$ is a model of exponential decay where a is the initial value, r is the decay rate, $1 - r$ is the decay factor, and t is the time period.

EXAMPLE **In 1999, 355 customers ate at Tom's Café every day, on average. Since then, the average number of customers who eat there each day has decreased at a rate of 4% per year.**

   a. Write a function that models the average daily number of customers who eat at the cafe over time.

   b. How many customers ate at Tom's café each day, on average, in 2003? Round your answer to the nearest whole number.

Solution:

   a. Let C be the average number of customers who eat at Tom's Café each day, and let t be the time (in years) since 1999. The initial value a is 355, and the decay rate r is 0.04.

        $W = a(1 - r)^t$ **Write exponential decay model.**

           $= 355(1 - 0.04)^t$ **Substitute 355 for a and 0.04 for r.**

           $= 355(0.96)^t$ **Simplify.**

   b. 2003 is 4 years after 1999. Substitute 4 for t.

        $W = 355(0.96)^4$ **Substitute 4 for t.**

          ≈ 302 **Use a calculator.**

In 2003, about 302 customers ate at the café each day.

PRACTICE **Solve.**

15. An essay contest starts with 95 entries. In each round of judging, the judges eliminate 25% of the essays.

   a. Write a function that models the number of essays in the contest over time.

   b. How many essays are still in the contest after 5 rounds of judging? Round your answer to the nearest whole number.

16. An oven is heated to 475°F and then turned off. The temperature of the oven decreases 8% per minute.

   a. Write a function that models the oven's temperature over time.

   b. What is the temperature of the oven after 15 minutes? Round your answer to the nearest whole degree.

Benchmark 4
(Chapters 7 and 8)

Quiz

Graph the function. Identify its domain and range.

1. $y = 10^x$

2. $y = \left(\frac{1}{7}\right)^x$

3. $y = \left(\frac{5}{3}\right)^x$

4. $y = (0.27)^x$

5. $y = (4.1)^x$

6. $y = (0.72)^x$

Solve.

7. In 1960, a museum bought a statue worth $5000. The statue's value has increased at a rate of 5.8% per year.

   a. Write a function that models the value of the statue over time.

   b. What was the value of the statue in 2005? Round your answer to the nearest whole dollar.

8. A chef makes an ice sculpture with 45 pounds of ice. As the sculpture melts, the weight of the remaining ice decreases by 2.5% per minute.

   a. Write a function that models the weight of the remaining ice over time.

   b. What is the weight of the remaining ice after 120 minutes? Round your answer to the nearest whole pound.

BENCHMARK 4
(Chapters 7 and 8)

C. Adding, Subtracting, and Multiplying Polynomials

Real numbers can be represented by **polynomials**. Polynomials can be added, subtracted, and multiplied. The result of any of these operations on polynomials is another polynomial.

1. Identify and Classify Polynomials

Vocabulary

Monomial A number, a variable, or the product of a number and one or more variables with whole number exponents.

Degree of a monomial The greatest sum of the exponents of the variables in a monomial.

Polynomial A monomial or a sum of monomials, each called a *term*.

Degree of a polynomial The greatest sum of the exponents of the variables in a monomial.

Binomial A polynomial with two terms.

Trinomial A polynomial with three terms.

EXAMPLE **Tell whether the expression is a polynomial. If it is a polynomial, find its degree and classify it by the number of its terms. Otherwise, tell why it is not a polynomial.**

An exponent of a variable in a polynomial must be a whole number.

	Expression	Is it a polynomial?	Classify by degree and number of terms
a.	7	Yes	0 degree monomial
b.	$3x^3 + 2x$	Yes	3rd degree binomial
c.	$4d^x - d^2 + 3$	No; variable exponent	
d.	$2x^{-4} + 3x^2$	No; negative exponent	
e.	$6m^3n - 5mn^2 - 1$	Yes	4th degree trinomial

PRACTICE **Tell whether the expression is a polynomial. If it is a polynomial, find its degree and classify it by the number of its terms. Otherwise, tell why it is not a polynomial.**

1. $5x$

2. $4x^a - 3x + 2$

3. $2z^4 + 5z^2$

4. $2ab^4 + 4a^2b - 1$

5. $3y^{-3} - y^2 - 4$

6. $4m^3 - 5m^2 + m - 7$

2. Add and Subtract Polynomials

EXAMPLE **Find the sum.**

When a power of the variable appears in one polynomial but not the other, leave a space in that column, or write the term with a coefficient of 0 as a placeholder.

a. $(4x^3 - 3x^2 + 2) + (x^2 + 2x - 3)$

b. $(4x^2 + 3x - 4) + (x^2 - 2x + 1)$

Solution:

a. **Vertical format:** Align the terms in vertical columns.

$$
\begin{array}{r}
4x^3 - 3x^2 \quad\;\; + 2 \\
+ \quad\quad x^2 + 2x - 3 \\
\hline
4x^3 - 2x^2 + 2x - 1
\end{array}
$$

BENCHMARK 4
(Chapters 7 and 8)

b. **Horizontal format:** Group like terms and simplify.

$$(4x^2 + 3x - 4) + (x^2 - 2x + 1) = (4x^2 + x^2) + [3x + (-2x)] + (-4 + 1)$$

$$= 5x^2 + x - 3$$

EXAMPLE

Find the difference.

To subtract a polynomial, add its opposite. Write the subtraction as addition, and multiply *each* term in the polynomial by -1.

a. $(3x^2 + 2) - (-x^2 + 3x - 1)$ **b.** $(2x^2 - 4x + 4) - (x^2 - x + 1)$

Solution:

a.
$$
\begin{array}{r}
3x^2 + 2 \\
(-) \ -x^2 + 3x - 1 \\
\end{array}
\qquad
\begin{array}{r}
3x^2 + 2 \\
+ \ x^2 - 3x + 1 \\
\hline
4x^2 - 3x + 3
\end{array}
$$

b. $(2x^2 - 4x + 4) - (x^2 - x + 1) = 2x^2 - 4x + 4 - x^2 + x - 1$

$$= (2x^2 - x^2) + (-4x + x) + (4 - 1)$$

$$= x^2 - 3x + 3$$

PRACTICE   **Find the sum or difference.**

7. $(2x^2 + 3x - 1) + (x^3 - 4x + 3)$ **8.** $(x^2 + 2) - (4x^2 + 5x - 3)$

9. $(3x^4 - 3x^2 + 5) + (2x^3 - x^2 + 2x - 3)$ **10.** $(5x^3 + 2x^2 - x + 1) - (x^3 - x^2 - 2)$

11. $(4x^2 + x - 6) - (2x^2 - 3x + 2)$ **12.** $(4x^2 + 3x - 4) + (x^2 - 2x + 1)$

3. Multiply Polynomials

EXAMPLE   **Find the product.**

a. $3x^2(2x^3 + x^2 - 3)$ **b.** $(2a^2 - a - 6)(5a + 2)$ **c.** $(y^2 - 3y + 4)(2y - 5)$

Solution:

a. $3x^2(2x^3 + x^2 - 3)$ Write product.

$= 3x^2(2x^3) + 3x^2(x^2) - 3x^2(3)$ **Distributive property**

$= 6x^5 + 3x^4 - 9x^2$ **Product of powers property**

b. **Step 1:** **Multiply** by 2.

$$
\begin{array}{r}
2a^2 - a - 6 \\
\times 5a + 2 \\
\hline
4a^2 - 2a - 12
\end{array}
$$

Align like terms vertically to help you add correctly.

Step 2: **Multiply** by $5a$.

$$
\begin{array}{r}
2a^2 - a - 6 \\
\times 5a + 2 \\
\hline
4a^2 - 2a - 12 \\
10a^3 - 5a^2 - 30a
\end{array}
$$

BENCHMARK 4
C. Polynomial Operations

BENCHMARK 4
(Chapters 7 and 8)

Step 3: Add products.

$$
\begin{array}{r}
2a^2 - a - 6 \\
\times 5a + 2 \\
\hline
4a^2 - 2a - 12 \\
10a^3 - 5a^2 - 30a \\
\hline
10a^3 - a^2 - 32a - 12
\end{array}
$$

c. $(y^2 - 3y + 4)(2y - 5)$ Write product.

     $= y^2(2y - 5) - 3y(2y - 5) + 4(2y - 5)$ Distributive property

     $= 2y^3 - 5y^2 - 6y^2 + 15y + 8y - 20$ Distributive property

     $= 2y^3 - 11y^2 + 23y - 20$ Combine like terms.

PRACTICE   **Find the product.**

13. $4b^3(2b^2 + b - 3)$ **14.** $2x^4(2x^3 - 5x^2 - x + 6)$

15. $(y^2 - 3y + 5)(2y - 1)$ **16.** $(2z - 3)(z^2 + 4z - 1)$

17. $(a^2 - 5a - 2)(2a - 3)$ **18.** $(3x + 2)(2x^2 - 3x + 4)$

4. Find Special Products of Polynomials

EXAMPLE   **Find the product.**

     a. $(2x + 5)^2$ **b.** $(3y - 2)^2$ **c.** $(2x + y)(2x - y)$

Solution:

$(a + b)^2 =$
$a^2 + 2ab + b^2$

     a. $(2x + 5)^2 = (2x)^2 + 2(2x)(5) + (5)^2$ Square of a binomial pattern
                $= 4x^2 + 20x + 25$ Simplify.

$(a - b)^2 =$
$a^2 - 2ab + b^2$

     b. $(3y - 2)^2 = (3y)^2 - 2(3y)(2) + (2)^2$ Square of a binomial pattern
                $= 9y^2 - 12y + 4$ Simplify.

$(a + b)(a - b)$
$= a^2 - b^2$

     c. $(2x + y)(2x - y) = (2x)^2 - y^2$ Sum and difference pattern
                       $= 4x^2 - y^2$ Simplify.

PRACTICE   **Find the product.**

19. $(2m + 5)^2$ **20.** $(z - 7)(z + 7)$ **21.** $(3x - 4)^2$

22. $(2x - 4)(2x + 4)$ **23.** $(2s + t)^2$ **24.** $(5x + 2)(5x - 2)$

BENCHMARK 4
C. Polynomial Operations

BENCHMARK 4
(Chapters 7 and 8)

Quiz

Tell whether the expression is a polynomial. If it is a polynomial, find its degree and classify it by the number of its terms. Otherwise, tell why it is not a polynomial.

1. $-6x^{-2}$ **2.** $3x + 1$ **3.** $x^3 + 2x^2 - 5x + 4$

4. $x^3 - 2x^2 + x^n - 7$ **5.** $3x^3 y^2 + 2x^2 y + xy$ **6.** $4x^2 - 3x + 1$

Evaluate the expression.

7. $(x^2 + 6x - 3) + (2x^3 - 2x + 5)$ **8.** $(5x^2 + 2x - 1) - (3x^2 - 4x + 2)$

9. $(x^2 + 3) - (-3x^2 - 2x + 6)$ **10.** $(2x^2 + x - 2) + (x^2 - 5x - 4)$

11. $3z^2(2z^3 - 4z + 5)$ **12.** $(5x + 1)(3x^2 - x - 7)$

13. $4b^3(b^3 - 2b^2 - 1)$ **14.** $(3y - 4)(3y + 4)$

15. $(k - 9)^2$ **16.** $(2x - 3)(x^2 + 5x - 2)$

17. $(2p + 3r)(2p - 3r)$ **18.** $(5x + 1)(2x - 3)$

19. $(3y + 5)^2$

BENCHMARK 4
(Chapters 7 and 8)

D. Factoring Polynomials

Polynomial equations can often be solved by **factoring**. To factor a polynomial, write it as a product of other polynomials. Then use the **zero-product property** to find the **roots** of the equation. The following examples describe methods that can be used to factor polynomial equations and find their solutions.

1. Use the Zero-Product Property

Vocabulary **Greatest common factor (GCF) of a polynomial** A monomial with an integer coefficient that divides evenly into each term of the polynomial.

Zero-Product Property Let a and b be real numbers. If $ab = 0$, then $a = 0$ or $b = 0$.

Roots The solutions of an equation in which one side is zero and the other side is a product of polynomial factors.

EXAMPLE **Solve $(x - 3)(x + 1) = 0$.**

$(x - 3)(x + 1) = 0$ Write original equation.

$x - 3 = 0 \text{ or } x + 1 = 0$ Zero-product property

$\quad x = 3 \text{ or } \qquad x = -2$ Solve for x.

PRACTICE **Use the zero-product property to solve the equation.**

1. $(x - 2)(x + 6) = 0$ **2.** $(x - 1)(x - 8) = 0$ **3.** $(x + 3)(x + 4) = 0$

2. Solve an Equation by Factoring

EXAMPLE **Solve the equation.**

     a. $3x^2 - 6x = 0$ **b.** $5a^2 = 25a$

Solution:

     a. $3x^2 - 6x = 0$ Write original equation.

         $3x(x - 2) = 0$ Factor left side.

         $3x = 0 \text{ or } x - 2 = 0$ Zero-product property

           $x = 0 \text{ or } \qquad x = 2$ Solve for x.

Write the equation so that one side is 0 in order to use the zero-product property.

     b. $15a^2 = 20a$ Write original equation.

         $15a^2 - 20a = 0$ Subtract $20a$ from each side.

         $5a(3a - 4) = 0$ Factor left side.

         $5a = 0 \text{ or } 3a - 4 = 0$ Zero-product property

           $a = 0 \text{ or } \qquad a = \dfrac{4}{3}$ Solve for a.

PRACTICE **Solve the equation by factoring.**

     4. $4b^2 - 16b = 0$ **5.** $x^2 + 7x = 0$ **6.** $8m^2 = -6m$

     7. $5z^2 = 7z$ **8.** $6a^2 - 3a = 0$ **9.** $10x^2 = 2x$

BENCHMARK 4
(Chapters 7 and 8)

3. Factor $x^2 + bx + c$

EXAMPLE

Factor the polynomial.

$x^2 + bx + c$
$= (x + p)(x + q)$
if $p + q = b$ and
$pq = c$.

a. $x^2 + 8x + 12$ **b.** $t^2 - 7t + 10$ **c.** $z^2 - 5z - 14$

Solution:

To find two
positive factors
of 12 whose sum
is 8, make an
organized list.

a.

Factors of 12	Sum of factors	
12, 1	$12 + 1 = 13$	✗
6, 2	$6 + 2 = 8$	← Correct sum
4, 3	$4 + 3 = 7$	✗

The factors 6 and 2 have a sum of 8, so they are the correct values of p and q.
$x^2 + 8x + 12 = (x + 6)(x + 2)$

Both p and q must
be negative, since
b is negative and
c is positive.

b.

Factors of 10	Sum of factors	
$-10, -1$	$-10 + (-1) = -11$	✗
$-5, -2$	$-5 + (-2) = -7$	← Correct sum

$t^2 - 7t + 10 = (x - 5)(x - 2)$

Since c is
negative, p and
q must have
different signs.

c.

Factors of −14	Sum of factors	
$-14, 1$	$-14 + 1 = -13$	✗
$14, -1$	$14 + (-1) = 13$	✗
$-7, 2$	$-7 + 2 = -5$	← Correct sum
$7, -2$	$7 + (-2) = 5$	✗

$z^2 - 5z - 14 = (x - 7)(x + 2)$

PRACTICE

Factor the polynomial.

10. $z^2 + 7z + 12$ **11.** $n^2 - 8n + 7$ **12.** $m^2 - 2m - 24$

13. $y^2 - 5y + 6$ **14.** $t^2 + 2t - 15$ **15.** $x^2 + 6x + 5$

4. Factor $ax^2 + bx + c$

EXAMPLE

Factor the polynomial.

a. $3x^2 - 5x + 2$ **b.** $2t^2 + t - 3$ **c.** $-5m^2 + 9m + 2$

Solution:

When a is positive,
consider the signs
of b and c. Since
b is negative and
c is positive, both
factors must be
negative.

a.

Factors of 3	Factors of 2	Possible factorization	Middle term when multiplied	
1, 3	$-1, -2$	$(x - 1)(3x - 2)$	$-2x - 3x = -5x$	← Correct
1, 3	$-2, -1$	$(x - 2)(3x - 1)$	$-x - 6x = -7x$	✗

$3x^2 - 5x + 2 = (x - 1)(3x - 2)$

BENCHMARK 4
(Chapters 7 and 8)

Since *b* is positive and *c* is negative, the factors of *c* must have different signs.

b.

Factors of 2	Factors of −3	Possible factorization	Middle term when multiplied	
1, 2	1, −3	$(t + 1)(2t − 3)$	$−3t + 2t = −t$	✗
1, 2	−1, 3	$(t − 1)(2t + 3)$	$3t − 2t = t$	← Correct
1, 2	3, −1	$(t + 3)(2t − 1)$	$−t + 6t = 5t$	✗
1, 2	−3, 1	$(t − 3)(2t + 1)$	$t − 6t = −5t$	✗

$2t^2 + t − 3 = (t − 1)(2t + 3)$

When *a* is negative, first factor −1 from each term of the trinomial. Then factor as in the previous examples.

Remember to include the −1 that you factored out earlier.

c. $−5m^2 + 9m + 2 = −(5m^2 − 9m − 2)$

Factors of 5	Factors of −2	Possible factorization	Middle term when multiplied	
1, 5	1, −2	$(m + 1)(5m − 2)$	$−2m + 5m = 3m$	✗
1, 5	2, −1	$(m + 2)(5m − 1)$	$−m + 10m = 9m$	✗
1, 5	−1, 2	$(m − 1)(5m + 2)$	$2m − 5m = −3m$	✗
1, 5	−2, 1	$(m − 2)(5m + 1)$	$m − 10m = −9m$	← Correct

$−5m^2 + 9m + 2 = −(m − 2)(5m + 1)$

PRACTICE **Factor the polynomial.**

16. $4x^2 − 8x − 5$ **17.** $2y^2 − 11y + 9$ **18.** $−4z^2 + 4z + 15$

19. $3m^2 − 10m + 8$ **20.** $−2x^2 + 17x − 21$ **21.** $3t^2 + 5t − 12$

5. Factor Special Products

EXAMPLE **Factor the polynomial.**

Difference of two squares: $a^2 − b^2 = (a + b)(a − b)$

a. $4x^2 − 25 = 0$ **b.** $4m^2 − 12m + 9$ **c.** $9z^2 + 30z + 25$

Solution:

a. $4x^2 − 25 = (2x)^2 − 5^2$ Write as $a^2 − b^2$.
$= (2x + 5)(2x − 5)$ Difference of two squares pattern

Perfect square trinomial:
$a^2 + 2ab + b^2 = (a + b)^2$
$a^2 − 2ab + b^2 = (a − b)^2$

b. $4m^2 − 12m + 9 = (2m)^2 − 2(2m \cdot 3) + 3^2$ Write as $a^2 − 2ab + b^2$.
$= (2m − 3)^2$ Perfect square trinomial pattern

c. $9z^2 + 30z + 25 = (3z)^2 + 2(3z \cdot 5) + 5^2$ Write as $a^2 + 2ab + b^2$.
$= (3z + 5)^2$ Perfect square trinomial pattern

PRACTICE **Factor the polynomial.**

22. $9x^2 − 1$ **23.** $4s^2 + 4s + 1$ **24.** $4m^2 − 12mn + 9n^2$

25. $16t^2 − 9$ **26.** $25z^2 − 20z + 4$ **27.** $x^2 + 8xy + 16y^2$

BENCHMARK 4
D. Factoring Polynomials

BENCHMARK 4
(Chapters 7 and 8)

6. Factor by Grouping

Vocabulary

Factor by grouping In a polynomial of four terms, factor a common monomial from pairs of terms, then look for a common binomial factor.

EXAMPLE

Check your factorization by multiplying the factors. Or graph the original polynomial and the factors on a graphing calculator. The two graphs should coincide.

Factor the polynomial.

a. $m^3 + 4m^2 - 3m - 12$ **b.** $s^2 + 2st - 2s - 4t$

Solution:

a.
$$\begin{aligned} m^3 + 4m^2 - 3m - 12 &= (m^3 + 4m^2) + (-3m - 12) && \text{Group terms.} \\ &= m^2(m + 4) + (-3)(m + 4) && \text{Factor each group.} \\ &= (m^2 - 3)(m + 4) && \text{Distributive property} \end{aligned}$$

b.
$$\begin{aligned} s^2 + 2st - 2s - 4t &= (s^2 + 2st) + (-2s - 4t) && \text{Group terms.} \\ &= s(s + 2t) + (-2)(s + 2t) && \text{Factor each group.} \\ &= (s - 2)(s + 2t) && \text{Distributive property} \end{aligned}$$

PRACTICE

Factor the polynomial.

28. $2t^3 + 3t^2 - 10t - 15$ **29.** $2m^2 - 10m + mn - 5n$

30. $3x^3 - 21x^2 + x - 7$ **31.** $x^2 - 4x + 2xy - 8y$

Quiz

Factor the polynomial.

1. $4y^3 - 20y$ **2.** $10m^4 + 15m^2$ **3.** $t^2 - 7t - 18$

4. $x^2 + 6x - 27$ **5.** $4s^2 - 27s - 7$ **6.** $10y^2 + 9y + 2$

7. $16x^4 - y^2$ **8.** $25s^2 - 4t^2$ **9.** $m^2 - 6mn + 9n^2$

10. $4x^2 + 24xy + 36y^2$ **11.** $x^2 + 4xy - 3x - 12y$ **12.** $t^2 + 3st - 2t - 6s$

Factor and use the zero-product property to solve the equation.

13. $2x^2 + 6x = 0$ **14.** $r^2 + r - 20 = 0$ **15.** $y^2 - 6y = 16$

16. $3x^2 = 5 - 14x$ **17.** $4m^2 - 8m + 3 = 0$ **18.** $z^2 = 64$

19. $9n^2 - 4 = 0$ **20.** $9x^2 + 30x + 25 = 0$ **21.** $4z^2 + 1 = 4z$

BENCHMARK 4
D. Factoring Polynomials

BENCHMARK 5
(Chapters 9, 10, and 11)

A. Graphing Quadratic Functions

A quadratic function is a nonlinear function that can be written in the **standard form** $y = ax^2 + bx + c$ where $a \neq 0$. The following examples describe how to graph quadratic functions, first where $b = 0$ and $c = 0$, then where $b = 0$, and finally where all three coefficients are nonzero. The examples also describe how to find certain characteristics of graphs of quadratic functions.

1. Graph $y = ax^2$

Vocabulary

Parent quadratic function The most basic quadratic function, $y = x^2$ as shown.

Parabola The U-shaped graph of a quadratic function.

Vertex The lowest or highest point on a parabola.

Axis of symmetry The line that passes through a parabola's vertex and divides the parabola into two symmetric parts.

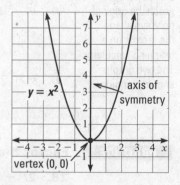

EXAMPLE **Graph the function. Compare the graph with the graph of $y = x^2$.**

a. $y = 2x^2$ **b.** $y = -\dfrac{1}{5}x^2$

Solution:

a. **Step 1:** **Make** a table of values for $y = 2x^2$.

x	-2	-1	0	1	2
y	8	2	0	2	8

Plot additional points if you are having trouble seeing the shape of the parabola with just five points.

Step 2: **Plot** the points from the table.

Step 3: **Draw** a smooth curve through the points.

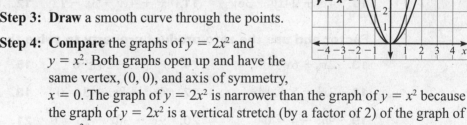

Step 4: **Compare** the graphs of $y = 2x^2$ and $y = x^2$. Both graphs open up and have the same vertex, $(0, 0)$, and axis of symmetry, $x = 0$. The graph of $y = 2x^2$ is narrower than the graph of $y = x^2$ because the graph of $y = 2x^2$ is a vertical stretch (by a factor of 2) of the graph of $y = x^2$.

b. **Step 1:** **Make** a table of values for $y = -\dfrac{1}{5}x^2$.

Choose values of x that result in whole numbers for y, whenever possible.

x	-5	-2	0	2	5
y	-5	-0.8	0	-0.8	-5

Step 2: **Plot** the points from the table.

Step 3: **Draw** a smooth curve through the points.

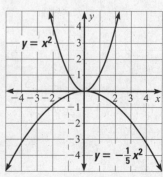

BENCHMARK 5
(Chapters 9, 10, and 11)

A parabola opens up when the coefficient of x^2 is positive and opens down when the coefficient of x^2 is negative.

Step 4: Compare the graphs of $y = -\frac{1}{5}x^2$ and $y = x^2$. Both graphs open up and have the same vertex, $(0, 0)$, and axis of symmetry, $x = 0$. However, the graph of $y = -\frac{1}{5}x^2$ is wider than the graph of $y = x^2$ and it opens down. This is because the graph of $y = -\frac{1}{5}x^2$ is a vertical shrink (by a factor of $\frac{1}{5}$) with a reflection in the x-axis of the graph of $y = x^2$.

PRACTICE Graph the function. Compare the graph with the graph of $y = x^2$.

1. $y = 4x^2$
2. $y = -\frac{1}{3}x^2$
3. $y = \frac{1}{2}x^2$

2. Graph $y = x^2 + c$

EXAMPLE Graph $y = x^2 + 3$. Compare the graph with the graph of $y = x^2$.

Step 1: Make a table of values for $y = x^2 + 3$.

x	-2	-1	0	1	2
y	7	4	3	4	7

Draw the x-axis and y-axis so that you have room to graph the points in your table.

Step 2: Plot the points from the table.

Step 3: Draw a smooth curve through the points.

Step 4: Compare the graphs of $y = x^2 + 3$ and $y = x^2$. Both graphs open up and have the same axis of symmetry, $x = 0$. However, the vertex of $y = x^2 + 3$, $(0, 3)$, is different than the vertex of the graph of $y = x^2$, $(0, 0)$, because the graph of $y = x^2 + 3$ is a vertical translation (of 3 units up) of the graph of $y = x^2$.

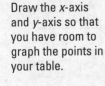

$y = x^2$ $y = x^2 + 3$

PRACTICE Graph the function. Compare the graph with the graph of $y = x^2$.

4. $y = x^2 + 1$
5. $y = x^2 - 2$
6. $y = x^2 + 4$

3. Find the Axis of Symmetry and the Vertex

EXAMPLE Consider the function $y = 2x^2 - 8x + 1$.

a. Find the axis of symmetry of the graph of the function.

b. Find the vertex of the graph of the function.

For the quadratic function $y = ax^2 + bx + c$, the **axis of symmetry** is $x = -\frac{b}{2a}$, and the **y-coordinate** of the **vertex** is $a\left(-\frac{b}{2a}\right)^2 + b\left(-\frac{b}{2a}\right) + c$

Solution:

a. For the function $y = 2x^2 - 8x + 1$, $a = 2$ and $b = -8$.

$x = -\frac{b}{2a} = -\frac{(-8)}{2(2)} = 2$ **Substitute 2 for a and -8 for b. Then simplify.**

b. The x-coordinate of the vertex is 2. To find the y-coordinate, substitute 2 for x in the function and find y.

$y = 2(2)^2 - 8(2) + 1 = -7$ **Substitute 2 for x. Then simplify.**

The vertex is $(2, -7)$.

BENCHMARK 5
(Chapters 9, 10, and 11)

PRACTICE   **Find the axis of symmetry and the vertex of the graph of the function.**

7. $y = x^2 + 2x + 9$ **8.** $2x^2 - 16x + 23$

9. $-3x^2 + 12x - 8$ **10.** $-x^2 - 4x - 7$

11. $4x^2 - 24x + 39$ **12.** $-2x^2 + 6x + 5$

EXAMPLE

4. Graph $y = ax^2 + bx + c$

Graph $y = x^2 - 4x + 3$.

Choose the location of the *x*-axis and *y*-axis so that you can easily graph the position in your table.

Step 1: Determine whether the parabola opens up or down. Because $a > 0$, the parabola opens up.

Step 2: Find and draw the axis of symmetry: $x = -\dfrac{b}{2a} = -\dfrac{-4}{2(1)} = 2$.

Step 3: Find and plot the vertex. The *x*-coordinate of the vertex is 2. To find the *y*-coordinate, substitute 2 for *x* in the function and simplify. $y = (2)^2 - 4(2) + 3 = -1$. So, the vertex is $(2, -1)$.

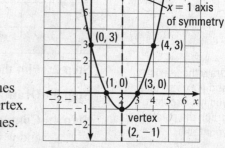

Step 4: Plot two points. Choose two *x*-values less than the *x*-coordinate of the vertex. Then find the corresponding *y*-values.

x	1	0
y	0	3

Step 5: Reflect the points plotted in Step 4 in the axis of symmetry.

Step 6: Draw a parabola through the plotted points.

Graph the function.

PRACTICE

13. $y = 2x^2 - 8x + 3$

14. $y = -3x^2 + 6x - 4$

15. $y = -x^2 - 10x - 20$

5. Find the Minimum or Maximum Value

Vocabulary

Minimum value The *y*-coordinate of the vertex of the function $y = ax^2 + bx + c$ when $a > 0$.

Maximum value The *y*-coordinate of the vertex of the function $y = ax^2 + bx + c$ when $a < 0$.

BENCHMARK 5
(Chapters 9, 10, and 11)

EXAMPLE **Tell whether the function $f(x) = 2x^2 - 4x + 5$ has a *minimum value* or a *maximum value*. Then find the minimum or maximum value.**

Because $a = 2$ and $2 > 0$, the parabola opens up and the function has a minimum value. To find the minimum value, find the vertex.

$x = -\dfrac{b}{2a} = -\dfrac{-4}{2(2)} = 1$ The x-coordinate is $-\dfrac{b}{2a}$.

$f(1) = 2(1)^2 - 4(1) + 5 = 3$ Substitute 1 for x. Then simplify.

The minimum value of the function is $f(1) = 3$.

PRACTICE **Tell whether the function has a *minimum value* or a *maximum value*. Then find the minimum or maximum value.**

16. $f(x) = -x^2 + 4x - 1$ **17.** $f(x) = 2x^2 - 6$

18. $f(x) = 3x^2 + 4$ **19.** $f(x) = -\dfrac{1}{2}x^2 + 2x + 3$

20. $f(x) = -5x^2 + 10x - 7$ **21.** $f(x) = 4x^2 + 8x$

Quiz

Graph the function. Label the vertex and the axis of symmetry.

1. $y = -3x^2$ **2.** $y = \dfrac{1}{2}x^2 - 2$ **3.** $y = 2x^2 - 4x + 5$

4. $y = x^2 - 4x$ **5.** $y = -2x^2 - 8x - 5$ **6.** $y = -x^2 - 4x - 7$

Tell whether the function has a *minimum value* or a *maximum value*. Then find the minimum or maximum value.

7. $f(x) = x^2 + 7$ **8.** $f(x) = -3x^2 - 6$

9. $f(x) = 2x^2 - x$ **10.** $f(x) = \dfrac{1}{2}x^2 - 4x + 1$

11. $f(x) = -2x^2 + 6x + 1$ **12.** $f(x) = -4x^2 - 8x + 3$

BENCHMARK 5
(Chapters 9, 10, and 11)

B. Solving Quadratic Equations

A quadratic equation is an equation that can be written in the **standard form** $ax^2 + bx + c = 0$ where $a \neq 0$. In Chapter 9 you used factoring to solve a quadratic equation. The following examples describe several additional methods you can use for solving quadratic equations.

1. Solve a Quadratic Equation by Graphing

Vocabulary   **Solutions, or roots, of a quadratic equation** The real numbers that make the equation true.

EXAMPLE   **Solve the quadratic equation by graphing.**

a. $x^2 + 3x = 4$ **b.** $-x^2 - 2x = 1$ **c.** $x^2 + 5 = x$

The *x*-intercepts of the related function $y = ax^2 + bx + c$ are the solutions, or roots, of $ax^2 + bx + c = 0.$

Solution:

a. **Step 1:** **Write** the equation in standard form.

$x^2 + 3x = 4$ **Write original equation.**

$x^2 + 3x - 4 = 0$ **Subtract 4 from each side.**

Step 2: **Graph** the function $y = x^2 + 3x - 4$.
The *x*-intercepts are -4 and 1.

The solutions of the equation $x^2 + 3x = 4$ are -4 and 1.

Check:

You can check -4 and 1 in the original equation.

$x^2 + 3x = 4$	$x^2 + 3x = 4$
$(-4)^2 + 3(-4) \stackrel{?}{=} 4$	$1^2 + 3(1) \stackrel{?}{=} 4$
$4 = 4$ ✔	$4 = 4$ ✔

Write original equation.
Substitute for *x*.
Simplify. Each solution checks.

b. **Step 1:** **Write** the equation in standard form.

$-x^2 - 2x = 1$ **Write original equation.**

$-x^2 - 2x - 1 = 0$ **Subtract 1 from each side.**

Step 2: **Graph** the function $y = -x^2 - 2x - 1$.
The *x*-intercept is -1.

The solution of the equation $-x^2 - 2x = 1$ is -1.

Although the graph has a *y*-intercept, only *x*-intercepts are solutions.

c. **Step 1:** **Write** the equation in standard form.

$x^2 + 5 = x$ **Write original equation.**

$x^2 - x + 5 = 0$ **Subtract *x* from each side.**

Step 2: **Graph** the function $y = x^2 - x + 5$.
The graph has no *x*-intercepts.

The equation $x^2 + 5 = x$ has no solution.

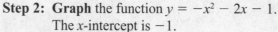
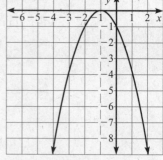
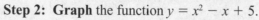
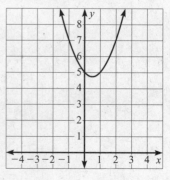

BENCHMARK 5
(Chapters 9, 10, and 11)

PRACTICE   Solve the quadratic equation by graphing.

1. $-x^2 + 2 = x$ **2.** $x^2 + 5x = -8$ **3.** $x^2 + 4x + 4 = 0$

4. $6x - 9 = x^2$ **5.** $-x^2 + 3x = 4$ **6.** $x^2 + x = 6$

2. Solve a Quadratic Equation Using Square Roots

EXAMPLE   Solve the equation.

  a. $-2x^2 = -18$ **b.** $c^2 + 5 = 5$ **c.** $t^2 + 6 = 2$

Solution:

  a. $-2x^2 = -18$ Write original equation.

  $x^2 = 9$ Divide each side by -2.

  $x = \pm\sqrt{9} = \pm 3$ Take square roots of each side. Simplify.

  b. $c^2 + 5 = 5$ Write original equation.

  $c^2 = 0$ Subtract 5 from each side.

  $c = 0$ The square root of 0 is 0.

Negative real numbers do not have real square roots.

  c. $t^2 + 6 = 2$ Write original equation.

  $t^2 = -4$ Subtract 6 from each side.

  There is no solution.

PRACTICE   Use square roots to solve the equation.

7. $y^2 + 12 = 12$ **8.** $-3t^2 = -27$ **9.** $m^2 + 10 = 4$

10. $x^2 - 2 = -11$ **11.** $x^2 - 5 = -5$ **12.** $2z^2 = 32$

3. Solve a Quadratic Equation by Completing the Square

Vocabulary   **Completing the square** The process of adding a constant c to an expression of the form $x^2 + bx$ so that the expression $x^2 + bx + c$ is a perfect square trinomial.

EXAMPLE   Solve $x^2 - 10x = 11$ by completing the square.

$x^2 + bx + \left(\dfrac{b}{2}\right)^2 =$

$\left(x + \dfrac{b}{2}\right)^2$

  $x^2 - 10x = 11$ Write original equation.

  $x^2 - 10x + (-5)^2 = 11 + (-5)^2$ Add $\left(\dfrac{-10}{2}\right)^2$, or $(-5)^2$ to each side.

  $(x - 5)^2 = 11 + (-5)^2$ Write left side as the square of a binomial.

  $(x - 5)^2 = 36$ Simplify the right side.

  $x - 5 = \pm 6$ Take square roots of each side.

  $x = 5 \pm 6$ Add 5 to each side.

The solutions of the equation are $5 + 6 = 11$ and $5 - 6 = -1$.

PRACTICE   Solve the quadratic equation by completing the square.

13. $x^2 + 4x = 12$ **14.** $x^2 + 2x = 3$ **15.** $x^2 - 2x = 35$

16. $x^2 + 12x = -32$ **17.** $x^2 - 6x = 27$ **18.** $x^2 + 16x = -39$

BENCHMARK 5
(Chapters 9, 10, and 11)

4. Solve a Quadratic Equation Using the Quadratic Formula

Vocabulary **The Quadratic Formula** The solutions of the quadratic equation.

$ax^2 + bx + c = 0$ are $x = \dfrac{-b \pm \sqrt{b^2 - 4ac}}{2a}$ when $a \neq 0$ and $b^2 - 4ac \geq 0$.

EXAMPLE **Solve $x^2 - 5 = 2x$.**

$x^2 - 5 = 2x$	Write original equation.
$x^2 - 2x - 5 = 0$	Write in standard form.
$x = \dfrac{-b \pm \sqrt{b^2 - 4ac}}{2a}$	Quadratic formula
$x = \dfrac{-(-2) \pm \sqrt{(-2)^2 - 4(1)(-5)}}{2(1)}$	Substitute values in the quadratic formula: $a = 1$, $b = -2$, and $c = -5$.
$x = \dfrac{2 \pm \sqrt{24}}{2} = 1 \pm \sqrt{6}$	Simplify.

Check your answer by graphing the related function on a graphing calculator. The *x*-intercepts should match your solutions.

The solutions are $1 + \sqrt{6} \approx 3.45$ and $1 - \sqrt{6} \approx -1.45$.

PRACTICE **Use the quadratic formula to solve the equation. Round your solutions to the nearest hundredth, if necessary.**

19. $x^2 + 4x = 7$ **20.** $3x^2 = 2x + 5$ **21.** $2x^2 + 3x = 1$

EXAMPLE **Tell what method(s) you would use to solve the quadratic equation.** *Explain* **your choice(s).**

    a. $x^2 = 8x$ **b.** $6x^2 - 22 = 0$ **c.** $3x^2 - 4x - 7 = 0$

Solution:

The quadratic formula can be used for *any* quadratic equation.

    a. The equation can be solved by factoring because the expression $x^2 - 8x$ can be factored easily. Also, the equation can be solved by completing the square because the equation is of the form $ax^2 + bx + c = 0$ where $a = 1$ and b is an even number.

    b. The quadratic equation can be solved using square roots because the equation can be written in the form $x^2 = d$.

    c. The quadratic equation cannot be factored easily, and completing the square will result in many fractions. So, the equation can be solved using the quadratic formula.

PRACTICE **Tell what method(s) you would use to solve the quadratic equation.** *Explain* **your choice(s).**

22. $2x^2 - x = 6$ **23.** $x^2 - 6x = 0$ **24.** $4x^2 + 2x - 9 = 0$

25. $-3x^2 = -54$ **26.** $x^2 - 3x = 6$ **27.** $x^2 - 4x = 3$

BENCHMARK 5
(Chapters 9, 10, and 11)

5. Solve Systems with Quadratic Equations

Vocabulary **System of linear equations** is of equations with the same variables.

Zero-product property states that for all numbers a and b, if $ab = 0$, then $a = 0$ or $b = 0$.

EXAMPLE **Solve the system of equations using the substitution method.**

$$y = 2x + 3 \qquad \text{Equation 1}$$
$$y = 2x^2 + 5x + 3 \qquad \text{Equation 2}$$

Solution:

Step 1: Solve one of the equations for y. The top equation is already solved for y.

Step 2: Substitute $2x + 3$ for y in the bottom equation and solve for x.

$y = 2x^2 + 5x + 3$	Write original Equation 2.
$2x + 3 = 2x^2 + 5x + 3$	Substitute $2x + 3$ for y.
$0 = 2x^2 + 3x$	Subtract $2x$ and 3 from each side.
$0 = x(2x + 3)$	Factor.
$x = 0$ or $2x + 3 = 0$	Zero-product property.
$x = 0$ or $x = -1.5$	Solve for x.

Step 3: Substitute both 0 and -1.5 for x in the top equation and solve for y.

$y = 2x + 3$	$y = 2x + 3$
$y = 2(0) + 3$	$y = 2(-1.5) + 3$
$y = 3$	$y = 0$

The solutions are $(0, 3)$ and $(-1.5, 0)$.

PRACTICE **Solve the system of equations using the substitution method.**

28. $y = x^2 + x - 6$
$y = x - 2$

29. $y = 2x^2 - 7x + 3$
$y = x - 3$

30. $y = -2x^2 + 4x + 2$
$y = -2x + 2$

Quiz

Solve the quadratic equation by graphing.

1. $x^2 + 16 = 8x$

2. $x^2 + 4x = -5$

3. $x^2 = x + 12$

Use square roots to solve the equation.

4. $t^2 + 5 = 9$

5. $m^2 + 8 = 0$

6. $y^2 + 7 = 7$

Solve the quadratic equation by completing the square.

7. $x^2 - 8x = 20$

8. $x^2 + 12x = 13$

9. $x^2 - 14x = -24$

Use the quadratic formula to solve the equation. Round your solutions to the nearest hundredth, if necessary.

10. $3x^2 + 1 = 5x$

11. $2x^2 + 2x = 5$

12. $x^2 - 2x - 7 = 0$

Solve the system of equations using the substitution method.

13. $y = 2x^2 + 3x - 4$
$y = x - 4$

14. $y = 4x^2 - 8$
$y = -4x$

15. $y = -3x^2 - 6x$
$y = 3$

Algebra 1

BENCHMARK 5
(Chapters 9, 10, and 11)

C. Comparing Linear, Exponential, and Quadratic Models

The linear, exponential, and quadratic functions you have studied can be used to model data. The following examples describe methods for determining which type of function best models a set of ordered pairs.

1. Choose Functions Using Sets of Ordered Pairs

EXAMPLE Use a graph to tell whether the ordered pairs represent a *linear function*, an *exponential function*, or a *quadratic function*.

a. $(-4, 10), (-2, 4), (0, 2), (2, 4), (4, 10)$ b. $(-4, 6), (-2, 4), (0, 2), (2, 0), (4, -2)$

c. $\left(-2, \frac{1}{27}\right), \left(-1, \frac{1}{9}\right), \left(0, \frac{1}{3}\right), (1, 1), (2, 3)$

Linear function:
$y = mx + b$

Exponential function: $y = ab^x$

Quadratic function: $y = ax^2 + bx + c$

Draw a smooth curve through the points you plot.

Solution:

a.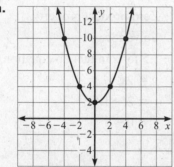

Quadratic function

b.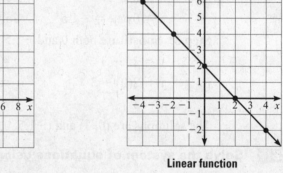

Linear function

c.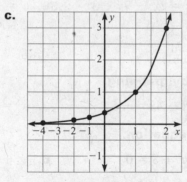

Exponential function

PRACTICE Use a graph to tell whether the ordered pairs represent a *linear function*, an *exponential function*, or a *quadratic function*.

1. $(-2, -1), (-1, 0), (0, 1), (1, 2), (2, 3)$

2. $\left(-2, \frac{3}{8}\right), \left(-1, \frac{3}{4}\right), \left(0, \frac{3}{2}\right), (1, 3), (2, 6)$

3. $(-2, 3), \left(-1, \frac{3}{2}\right), (0, 1), \left(1, \frac{3}{2}\right), (2, 3)$

Algebra 1

BENCHMARK 5
(Chapters 9, 10, and 11)

2. Model Relationships

EXAMPLE A car is traveling down a road. The distance from the beginning of the road is shown in the table below.

Time (s)	0	1	2	3	4	5
Distance (ft)	35	85	135	185	235	285

  a. What type of graph would best represent this situation?

  b. Sketch a graph representing the situation.

  c. What does the *y*-intercept represent?

Solution:

  a. Determine the relationship between the change in *y*-values for each interval. By subtracting each subsequent distance from the current one we can see it changes by the same amount. When *y*-values increase or decrease by the same amount it is a linear relationship, so the graph should be a line.

  b. Fill in the values from the standard form of a linear equation to get the equation of the line. At time = 0, the distance = 35. This is the *y*-intercept and the *b* of the standard equation.

  By taking any two points we can find the slope (*m*) of the equation: $\frac{85 - 35}{1 - 0} = \frac{50}{1} = 50$

  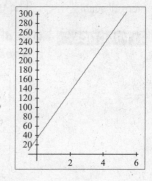

  The slope (*m*) of the line is 50. Putting these numbers into the standard form we can get the linear equation: $y = 50x + 35$. Using this we can sketch a graph of the line.

  c. Determine what the *x* = 0 means in this situation. When the time is 0 that is the start time for the distance the car travels. Therefore when the collection of data started the car was already at 35 ft from the beginning of the road. The *y*-intercept represents the distance from the beginning of the road at the start of the data collection.

PRACTICE **Determine which type of graph would best represent the given situation.**

  4. The amount of interest gained in a bank account.

  5. The temperature change over time of a pot of water being heated.

  6. The speed of a ball thrown up into the air.

  7. The thickness of a wedge of wood going from one end to the other.

BENCHMARK 5
(Chapters 9, 10, and 11)

3. Identify Functions Using Differences or Ratios

EXAMPLE

The table of values represents:

- an **exponential function** if the *ratios* of successive *y*-values are all equal
- a **linear function** if the *differences* of successive *y*-values are all equal
- a **quadratic function** if the *second differences* are all equal

Use differences or ratios to tell whether the table of values represents a *linear function*, an *exponential function*, or a *quadratic function*.

a.

x	−1	0	1	2	3
y	0.0625	0.25	1	4	16

Ratios: $\dfrac{0.25}{0.0625} = 4$ 4   4   4

Exponential function

b.

x	−1	0	1	2	3
y	1	3	5	7	9

Differences: 2   2   2   2

Linear function

c.

x	−1	0	1	2	3
y	4	2	4	10	20

First differences: −2   2   6   10

Second differences: 4   4   4

The table of values represents a quadratic function.

PRACTICE

Use differences or ratios to tell whether the table of values represents a *linear function*, an *exponential function*, or a *quadratic function*.

8.

x	−1	0	1	2	3
y	−3	0	3	6	9

9.

x	−1	0	1	2	3
y	7	4	3	4	7

10.

x	−1	0	1	2	3
y	0.5	2	8	32	128

4. Write an Equation for the Function

EXAMPLE

Check your function by plotting the ordered pairs from the table on the same grid as a graph of the function. The graph should pass through the plotted points.

Tell whether the table of values represents a *linear function*, an *exponential function*, or a *quadratic function*. Then write an equation for the function.

x	−2	−1	0	1	2
y	16	4	0	4	16

Step 1: Determine which type of function the table of values represents.

x	−2	−1	0	1	2
y	16	4	0	4	16

First differences: −12 −4   4   12

Second differences: 8   8   8

The table of values represents a quadratic function because the second differences are equal.

BENCHMARK 5
(Chapters 9, 10, and 11)

Step 2: Write an equation for the quadratic function. The equation has the form $y = ax^2$. Find the value of a by using the coordinates of a point that lies on the graph, such as $(1, 4)$.

$y = ax^2$	**Write equation for quadratic function.**
$4 = a(1)^2$	**Substitute 1 for x and 4 for y.**
$4 = a$	**Solve for a.**

The equation is $y = 4x^2$.

PRACTICE | **Tell whether the table of values represents a *linear function*, an *exponential function*, or a *quadratic function*. Then write an equation for the function.**

11.

x	−1	0	1	2	3
y	0.2	0	0.2	0.8	1.8

12.

x	−2	−1	0	1	2
y	−8	−5	−2	1	4

13.

x	−1	0	1	2	3
y	1	3	5	7	9

14.

x	−2	−1	0	1	2
y	12	3	0	3	12

Quiz

Use a graph to tell whether the ordered pairs represent a *linear function*, an *exponential function*, or a *quadratic function*.

1. $(−4, 9)$, $(−2, 3)$, $(0, 1)$, $(2, 3)$, $(4, 9)$

2. $(−4, −10)$, $(−2, −4)$, $(0, 2)$, $(2, 8)$, $(4, 14)$

3. $(−4, 0.0625)$, $(−2, 0.25)$, $(0, 1)$, $(2, 4)$, $(4, 16)$

4. A company is keeping track of their production costs per number of units made. For each additional unit they manufacture, the price of materials is cheaper than the previous unit.

   a. What type of graph represents this situation?

   b. What does the y-intercept represent?

BENCHMARK 5
(Chapters 9, 10, and 11)

Use differences or ratios to tell whether the table of values represents a *linear function*, an *exponential function*, or a *quadratic function*.

5.

x	−1	0	1	2	3
y	−3	2	7	12	17

6.

x	−1	0	1	2	3
y	$\frac{1}{9}$	$\frac{1}{3}$	1	3	9

7.

x	−1	0	1	2	3
y	6	3	4	9	18

Tell whether the table of values represents a *linear function*, an *exponential function*, or a *quadratic function*. Then write an equation for the function.

8.

x	−1	0	1	2	3
y	−3	−1	1	3	5

9.

x	−2	−1	0	1	2
y	16	4	0	4	16

10.

x	−1	0	1	2	3
y	0.1	0	0.1	0.4	0.9

11.

x	−2	−1	0	1	2
y	−6	−2	2	6	10

BENCHMARK 5
(Chapters 9, 10, and 11)

D. Analyzing Data

A **survey** is a study of one or more characteristics of a group, or **population**. Once data on a population is collected, it can be analyzed using **measures of central tendency** and **measures of dispersion**. Data can also be displayed in graphs of different types. The examples below describe these methods of analyzing and displaying data.

1. Classify a Sampling Method

Vocabulary

Remember that when a person or object is chosen *at random*, all choices are equally likely.

Sample Part of a population that is surveyed; Sample types:

Random Every member of the population has an equal chance of being selected.

Stratified random The population is divided into distinct groups; members are selected at random from each group.

Systematic A rule is used to select members of the population.

Convenience Only members of the population who are easily accessible are selected.

Self-selected Members of the population select themselves by volunteering.

EXAMPLE **Every fifth person who makes a purchases at a clothing store is asked to fill out a survey on their fashion preferences. Identify the population and classify the sampling method.**

Solution:

The population is all customers of the store who make a purchase. Because the rule *every fifth person* is used to select which customers are surveyed, the sample is a systematic sample.

PRACTICE **Identify the population and classify the sampling method.**

1. Five students from each homeroom of a school are chosen at random for a health survey.

2. Every voter in the county is mailed a survey on local tax issues.

3. Members of an environmental organization are phoned at random for a recycling survey.

2. Identify Bias

Vocabulary

Biased sample A sample that is not representative of the population.

Biased question A question that encourages a particular response.

EXAMPLE **In the previous example, suppose that surveys are only given to customers who purchase items made by one clothing manufacturer. Is this method likely to result in a biased sample?**

Solution:

Customers who purchase clothing from other manufacturers may hold significantly different opinions on fashion, so the method may result in a biased sample.

Algebra 1

BENCHMARK 5
(Chapters 9, 10, and 11)

EXAMPLE

Watch for biased phrases, such as "don't you think" and "isn't it true," and adjectives that are used to create bias.

Tell whether the question is potentially biased. Explain your answer. If the question is potentially biased, rewrite it so that it is not.

a. Do you think the city should create a lovely new park or a traffic-congesting shopping mall on the vacant land?

This question is biased because it suggests that a shopping mall will increase traffic congestion. An unbiased question is "Should the city create a new park or a new shopping mall on the vacant land?"

b. Isn't it safer for 17-year-olds to not be allowed to drive after 10:00 PM?

This question is biased because it suggests that 17-year-old drivers are unsafe after 10:00 PM. An unbiased question is "Should 17-year-old drivers be allowed to drive after 10:00 PM?"

PRACTICE

In a survey about students' interest in fitness, the members of the basketball teams were asked, "Isn't it important to participate in a school sport in order to stay fit?"

4. Is the sampling method likely to result in a biased sample? Explain.

5. Is the question potentially biased? Explain your answer. If the question is potentially biased, rewrite it so that it is not.

3. Compare Measures of Central Tendency

Vocabulary

The median of a data set with an even number of values is the mean of the two middle values.

Mean For the data set $x_1, x_2, ..., x_n$ the mean, or *average*, is

$$\bar{x} = \frac{x_1 + x_2 + \cdots + x_n}{n}.$$

Median The middle number of a numerical data set when the values are written in numerical order.

Mode The value of a data set is that occurs most frequently; there may be one, more than one, or no mode.

EXAMPLE

The daily high temperatures (in degrees Fahrenheit) for a city during one week are listed below. Which measure of central tendency best represents the data?

Solution:

35, 35, 45, 48, 64, 69, 75

$$\bar{x} = \frac{35 + 35 + 45 + 48 + 64 + 67 + 75}{7} = \frac{371}{7} = 53$$

The median is 48. The mode is 35.

The mean best represents the data. The mode is significantly less than most of the data. The mean and median both fall near the middle of the data, but the median is much closer to the lowest value than the highest value.

Copyright © by McDougal Littell, a division of Houghton Mifflin Company.

BENCHMARK 5
(Chapters 9, 10, and 11)

PRACTICE **The wingspans (in inches) of the birds in the zoo's raptor exhibit are listed below.**

10, 10, 39, 41, 42, 46, 48, 52

6. Find the mode of the data.

7. Find the median of the data.

8. Find the mean of the data.

9. Which measure of central tendency best represents the data?

4. Compare Measures of Dispersion

Vocabulary **Measure of dispersion** A measure which describes the dispersion, or spread, of data.

Range The range of a numerical data set is the difference of the greatest value and the least value. The range gives the length of the interval containing the data.

Mean absolute deviation The mean absolute deviation gives the average variation of the data from the mean. The mean absolute deviation of the data set $x_1, x_2, ..., x_n$ is given by:

$$\text{Mean absolute deviation} = \frac{|x_1 - \bar{x}| + |x_2 - \bar{x}| + \cdots + |x_n - \bar{x}|}{n}$$

EXAMPLE **The top 10 finishing times (in seconds) for runners in two women's races are given. The times in a 100 meter dash are in set A, and the times in a 200 meter dash are in set B. Compare the spread of the data for the two sets using (a) the range and (b) the mean absolute deviation.**

A: 12.75, 12.85, 12.86, 13.03, 13.17, 13.20, 13.37, 13.44, 13.56, 13.61

B: 24.00, 24.48, 25.09, 25.34, 25.61, 26.14, 26.29, 26.96, 27.11, 27.38

Some of the values in the mean absolute deviation formula signs will be negative. Remember that if a is negative, then $|a| = -a$.

a. A: $13.61 - 12.75 = 0.86$ B: $27.38 - 24.00 = 3.38$

The range of set B is greater than the range of set A. So, the data in B cover a wider interval than the data in A.

b. The mean of set A is 13.184, so the mean absolute deviation is:

$$\frac{|12.75 - 13.184| + |12.85 - 13.184| + \cdots + |13.61 - 13.184|}{10} = 0.252.$$

The mean of set B is 25.84, so the mean absolute deviation is:

$$\frac{|24.00 - 25.84| + |24.48 - 25.84| + \cdots + |27.38 - 25.84|}{10} = 0.936.$$

The mean absolute deviation of set B is greater, so the average variation from the mean is greater for the data is B than for the data is A.

BENCHMARK 5
(Chapters 9, 10, and 11)

PRACTICE The top 10 finishing times (in seconds) for runners in two 400 meter races are given. The times for the women's race are in set *A*, and the times for the men's race are in set *B*.

A: 59.0, 59.3, 59.4, 60.1, 60.6, 60.6, 61.0, 61.0, 61.7, 62.2

B: 50.9, 51.1, 51.2, 51.4, 51.6, 51.6, 51.9, 52.0, 52.3, 52.5

10. Compare the spread of the data for the two sets using the range.

11. Compare the spread of the data for the two sets using the mean absolute deviation.

5. Make a Stem-and-Leaf Plot

Vocabulary

A stem-and-leaf plot shows how data are distributed.

Stem-and-leaf plot A data display that organizes data based on their digits. Each value is separated into a *stem* (the leading digit(s)) and a *leaf* (the last digit). The plot also has a key that tells you how to read the data.

EXAMPLE **The final scores for a basketball team in 20 games are listed below. Make a stem-and-leaf plot of the data.**

Each stem defines an interval. For example, the stem 4 represents the interval 40–49, The data values in this interval are 44, 46, and 49.

65, 59, 63, 72, 84, 70, 51, 46, 50, 44, 66, 49, 58, 62, 77, 82, 73, 55, 63, 61

Solution:

Step 1: **Separate** the data into stems and leaves.

Final Scores

Stem	Leaves
4	6 4 9
5	9 1 0 8 5
6	5 3 6 2 3 1
7	2 0 7 3
8	4 2

Key: 6 | 5 = 65 points

Step 2: **Write** the leaves in increasing order.

Final Scores

Stem	Leaves
4	4 6 9
5	0 1 5 8 9
6	1 2 3 3 5 6
7	0 2 3 7
8	2 4

Key: 6 | 5 = 65 points

PRACTICE **The scores for 20 players in a charity golf tournament are listed below.**

101, 113, 82, 96, 74, 106, 102, 94, 110, 91, 105, 115, 78, 109, 114, 105, 97, 80, 94, 112

12. Make a stem-and-leaf plot of the data.

13. Describe the distribution of the data on the intervals represented by the stems. Are the data clustered together in a noticeable way? Explain.

BENCHMARK 5
(Chapters 9, 10, and 11)

6. Make a Histogram

Vocabulary

Since intervals have equal size, the bars of a histogram have equal width. There is no space between bars.

Frequency The number of data values in an interval.

Frequency table Groups data values into equal intervals, with no gaps between intervals and no intervals overlapping.

Histogram A bar graph that displays data from a frequency table. Each bar represents an interval. A bar's length indicates the frequency.

EXAMPLE **The prices (in dollars) of paperback books at a book fair are listed below. Make a histogram of the data.**

5.25, 5.50, 5.75, 5.75, 6.25, 6.50, 7.00, 7.00, 7.25, 7.75, 7.75, 8.25

Solution:

Choose the interval size for the frequency by dividing the range of the data by the number of intervals you want in the table. Use the quotient as an approximate interval size.

Step 1: **Choose** intervals of equal size that cover all of the data values. Organize the data using a frequency table.

Price	Books
$5.00–5.99	IIII
$6.00–6.99	II
$7.00–7.99	IIIII
$8.00–8.99	I

Step 2: Draw the bars of the histogram using the intervals from the frequency table.

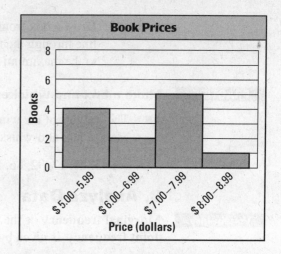

PRACTICE **Make a histogram.**

14. The average monthly high temperatures (in degrees Fahrenheit) of San Jose, California, are 59, 63, 67, 72, 77, 82, 84, 84, 82, 76, 65, and 59. Make a histogram of the data.

7. Make a Box-and-Whisker Plot

Vocabulary

Ordered data is divided into two halves by the median.

Lower quartile The median of the lower half of ordered data.

Upper quartile The median of the upper half of ordered data.

Box-and-whisker plot A plot that organizes data values into four groups divided by the lower quartile, the median, and the upper quartile.

EXAMPLE **The lengths of movies (in minutes) playing at a theater are listed below. Make a box-and-whisker plot of the movie lengths.**

132, 95, 86, 89, 105, 117, 128, 101, 107, 101, 127

BENCHMARK 5
(Chapters 9, 10, and 11)

Solution:

Step 1: Order the data. Then find the median and the quartiles.

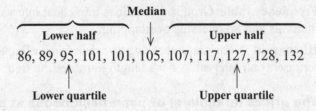

Step 2: Plot the median, the quartiles, the maximum value, and the minimum value below a number line.

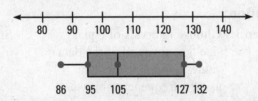

Step 3: Draw a box from the lower quartile to the upper quartile. Draw a vertical line through the median. Draw a line segment (a "whisker") from the box to the maximum and another from the box to the minimum.

PRACTICE   **Make a box-and-whisker plot.**

15.   The weights of the winning dogs in a dog show (in pounds) are listed below. Make a box-and-whisker plot of the weights.

65, 43, 24, 17, 92, 86, 54, 36, 29, 47, 61

8. Analyze Data

Vocabulary   **Marginal frequency** is the total of each row or column of a two-way frequency table. **Joint frequency** is given by the body of a two-way frequency table.

EXAMPLE   **The table shows the number of medals that the top three countries won in the 2008 Summer Olympic Games.**

	Gold	Silver	Bronze	Total
United States	36	38	36	110
China	51	21	28	100
Russia	23	21	28	72
Total	110	80	92	282

a.   Which type of medal did these three countries combined win the most?

b.   Is it true that the country that won the most gold medals also won the most medals?

Solution

a.   Look at the marginal frequencies in the Total row. The medal that had the greatest number was gold.

BENCHMARK 5
(Chapters 9, 10, and 11)

b. No. Even though the joint frequencies show that China won the greatest number of gold medals, the marginal frequencies show that the United States won the greatest number of medals.

PRACTICE The table shows the number of each type of ticket that was sold for three concerts.

	Pit	Orchestra	Balcony	Total
Show 1	85	120	154	359
Show 2	110	95	138	343
Show 3	76	152	183	411
Total	271	367	475	1113

16. Which show had the greatest number of tickets sold?

17. Did one type of ticket have the least number of tickets sold for more than one show? If so, which type of ticket and for which shows?

18. How many more balcony seats were sold than pit seats in all?

Quiz

Identify the population and classify the sampling method.

1. The first 50 people to arrive at a concert are given a music survey.

2. Every company employee born in July is given a carpool survey.

In a survey about violent content in movies, patrons of an action film were asked, "Don't you agree that violence in movies is merely harmless entertainment?"

3. Is the sampling method likely to result in a biased sample? Explain.

4. Is the question potentially biased? Explain your answer. If the question is potentially biased, rewrite it so that it is not.

The normal rainfall for 8 major California cities (in inches) is listed below.

6, 11, 11, 15, 22, 31, 33, 38

5. Find the mode of the data.

6. Find the median of the data.

7. Find the mean of the data.

8. Which measure of central tendency best represents the data?

BENCHMARK 5
(Chapters 9, 10, and 11)

The top 10 heights (in inches) for high jumpers at a track meet are given. The heights jumped by the women are in set *A*, and the heights jumped by the men are in set *B*.

A: 66, 64, 62, 62, 60, 60, 58, 56, 56, 54

B: 74, 74, 72, 72, 70, 68, 66, 66, 66, 64

9. Compare the spread of the data for the two sets using the range.

10. Compare the spread of the data for the two sets using the mean absolute deviation.

The final scores for a football team in 20 games are listed below.

31, 14, 7, 34, 3, 10, 17, 13, 27, 21, 35, 41, 24, 21, 3, 7, 26, 20, 19, 10

11. Make a stem-and-leaf plot of the data.

12. Describe the distribution of the data on the intervals represented by the stems. Are the data clustered together in a noticeable way? Explain.

Plot the data.

13. The average monthly high temperatures (in degrees Fahrenheit) of Austin, Texas, are 60, 65, 73, 79, 85, 91, 95, 96, 90, 81, 70, and 62. Make a histogram of the data.

14. The test scores for a science class are listed below. Make a box-and-whisker plot of the data.

78, 92, 97, 83, 64, 69, 77, 99, 55, 68, 86

Quiz

The table shows the scores each person bowled.

	Game 1	Game 2	Game 3	Total
Glenn	137	146	129	412
Jamal	153	118	162	433
Norb	124	163	132	419
Total	414	427	423	1264

15. Who had the greatest score after 3 games?

16. Did anyone win more than one game? If so, who and which games?

17. What was the difference between the best one-game score and the worst one-game score?

BENCHMARK 5
(Chapters 9, 10, and 11)

E. Probabilities of Simple and Compound Events

The **probability of an event** is a measure of the likelihood that the event will occur. The following examples describe how to find a **theoretical probability** and **odds** of an event occurring, and how to find the probabilities of **compound** events that are **independent** and **dependent**.

1. Find a Theoretical Probability

Vocabulary

Outcome A possible result of an experiment.

Event An outcome or a collection of outcomes.

Sample space The set of all possible outcomes.

Favorable outcomes The outcomes for a specified event.

Theoretical probability When all outcomes are equally likely, the theoretical probability $P(A)$ of event A is found by: $P(A) = \dfrac{\text{Number of favorable outcomes}}{\text{Total number of outcomes}}$

EXAMPLE

A bag contains 5 red, 6 blue, 4 green, and 9 yellow marbles. A student reaches in the bag and chooses a marble at random. What is the probability that the student chooses a yellow marble?

When an object is chosen *at random*, all choices are equally likely.

Solution:

The bag holds a total of $5 + 6 + 4 + 9 = 24$ marbles. So, there are 24 possible outcomes. Of all the marbles, 9 are yellow. There are 9 favorable outcomes.

$$P(\text{yellow marble}) = \frac{\text{Number of favorable outcomes}}{\text{Total number of outcomes}}$$

$$= \frac{\text{Number of yellow marbles}}{\text{Total number of marbles}} = \frac{9}{24} = \frac{3}{8}$$

PRACTICE

A soccer coach has a box that contains 3 small, 6 medium, 7 large, and 4 extra-large soccer jerseys. A player chooses a jersey at random. Find the probability that the player chooses a jersey of the given size.

1. small   **2.** medium   **3.** large   **4.** extra-large

2. Find the Odds

Vocabulary

Odds are read as the ratio of one number to another. The odds here are read as "five to one." Odds are usually written as $a : b$.

Odds The odds of an event compare the number of favorable and unfavorable outcomes when all outcomes are equally likely.

$$\text{Odds in favor} = \frac{\text{Number of favorable outcomes}}{\text{Number of unfavorable outcomes}}$$

$$\text{Odds against} = \frac{\text{Number of unfavorable outcomes}}{\text{Number of favorable outcomes}}$$

BENCHMARK 5
(Chapters 9, 10, and 11)

EXAMPLE **A number cube is rolled. Find the odds against a 4 being rolled.**

Solution:

The 6 possible outcomes are all equally likely. The one favorable outcome is a roll of 4. Rolling the other numbers are unfavorable outcomes.

$$\text{Odds against rolling a 4} = \frac{\text{Number of unfavorable outcomes}}{\text{Number of favorable outcomes}} = \frac{5}{1} \text{ or } 5:1$$

PRACTICE **A standard deck of 52 cards is shuffled and a card is drawn at random. Find the odds in favor of and against each of the following events.**

5. a red ace is drawn

6. a 6 is drawn

7. a spade is drawn

8. a face card is drawn

3. Use the Permutation Formula

Vocabulary ***n* factorial** For any positive integer n, the product of the integers from 1 to n, written as $n!$

Permutation An arrangement of objects in which order is important;

number of permutations of n objects: $_nP_n = n!$

number of permutations of n objects taken r at a time, where $r \le n$:

$$_nP_r = \frac{n!}{(n-r)!}$$

EXAMPLE **You borrow 10 books from the school library for a research project. You can only fit 4 in your backpack, so you leave the rest in the classroom. In how many ways can you arrange the remaining books on a classroom bookshelf?**

Solution:

To find the number of permutations of 6 books chosen from 10, find $_{10}P_6$.

Expand the factorial only as far as necessary. In this case, 4! is a factor of 10!.

$$_{10}P_6 = \frac{10!}{(10-6)!} \qquad \text{Permutations formula}$$

$$= \frac{10!}{4!} \qquad \text{Subtract.}$$

$$= \frac{10 \cdot 9 \cdot 8 \cdot 7 \cdot 6 \cdot 5 \cdot 4!}{4!} \qquad \begin{array}{l}\text{Expand factorials.}\\ \text{Divide out common factor, 4!.}\end{array}$$

$$= 151,200 \qquad \text{Multiply.}$$

There are 151,200 ways to arrange 6 books out of 10.

PRACTICE **Find the number of ways you can arrange the number of letters in the word.**

9. DOG, 2 of the letters

10. ORANGE, 4 of the letters

11. JULY, 3 of the letters

12. PICTURE, 6 of the letters

BENCHMARK 5
(Chapters 9, 10, and 11)

4. Use the Combination Formula

Vocabulary

Combination A selection of objects in which order is not important; number of combinations of n objects taken r at a time, where $r \leq n$:

$$_nC_r = \frac{n!}{(n-r)! \cdot r!}$$

You order a sundae at a yogurt shop. You can choose 3 toppings from a list of 9. How many combinations of toppings are possible?

Solution:

The order in which you choose the toppings is not important. So, to find the number of combinations of 9 toppings taken 3 at a time, find $_9C_3$.

$$_9C_3 = \frac{9!}{(9-3)! \cdot 3!} \qquad \text{Permutations formula}$$

$$= \frac{9!}{6! \cdot 3!} \qquad \text{Subtract.}$$

$$= \frac{9 \cdot 8 \cdot 7 \cdot 6!}{6! \cdot (3 \cdot 2 \cdot 1)} \qquad \begin{array}{l}\text{Expand factorials.}\\ \text{Divide out common factor, 6!.}\end{array}$$

$$= 84 \qquad \text{Simplify.}$$

There are 84 different combinations of toppings you can choose.

PRACTICE

A pizza shop offers a daily special where customers can choose a number of toppings from a list of toppings available that day. Find the number of possible combinations for each daily special.

13. choose 2 toppings from 6 toppings   **14.** choose 3 toppings from 8 toppings

15. choose 1 topping from 5 toppings   **16.** choose 4 toppings from 10 toppings

5. Find the Probability of a Compound Event

Vocabulary

Compound event A combination of two or more events, using the word *and* or the word *or*.

Mutually exclusive events Events that have no common outcomes:

$P(A \text{ or } B) = P(A) + P(B)$.

Overlapping events Events that have at least one common outcome:

$P(A \text{ or } B) = P(A) + P(B) - P(A \text{ and } B)$.

EXAMPLE

Draw a Venn diagram to help you understand mutual and overlapping events.

You roll a number cube. Find the probability that you roll a number greater than 4 or an odd number.

Solution:

Because 5 is both a number greater than 4 and an odd number, rolling a number greater than 4 and an odd number are overlapping events. There are 2 numbers greater than 4, 3 odd numbers, and 1 number that is both.

$P(\text{greater than 4 or odd}) = P(\text{greater than 4}) + P(\text{odd}) - P(\text{greater than 4 and odd})$

$$= \frac{2}{6} + \frac{3}{6} - \frac{1}{6} = \frac{4}{6} = \frac{2}{3}$$

BENCHMARK 5
(Chapters 9, 10, and 11)

PRACTICE   **You roll a number cube. Find the probability of each outcome.**

17.   a number less than 4 or an odd number

18.   a multiple of 3 or a prime number

19.   an odd number or a number greater than 3

6. Find the Probability of Independent and Dependent Events

Vocabulary   **Independent events** Two events are independent events if the occurrence of one event has no effect on the occurrence of the other. $P(A$ and $B) = P(A) \cdot P(B)$.

Dependent events Two events are dependent events if the occurrence of one event affects the occurrence of the other. $P(A$ and $B) = P(A) \cdot P(B$ given $A)$.

EXAMPLE   **A box contains 6 red markers and 3 green markers. You choose one marker at random, do not replace it, then choose a second marker at random. What is the probability that both markers are red?**

After one item is chosen and not replaced, reduce the total number remaining by 1.

Solution:

Because you do not replace the first marker, the events are dependent. Before you choose a marker, there are 9 markers, and 6 of them are red. After you choose a red marker, there are 8 markers left, and 5 of them are red.

$P(\text{red and then red}) = P(\text{red}) \cdot P(\text{red given red})$

$$= \frac{6}{9} \cdot \frac{5}{8} = \frac{30}{72} = \frac{5}{12}$$

PRACTICE   **A bag contains 5 blue, 4 red, and 3 green marbles. You randomly draw 2 marbles, one at a time. Find the probability:**

20.   of drawing a red marble, which you replace, and then drawing a green marble

21.   of drawing two blue marbles without replacement

22.   of drawing a green marble, which you do not replace, and then drawing a blue marble

Quiz

A jar on a store counter contains pens of 5 different colors. The jar contains 6 red pens, 8 blue pens, 4 green pens, 10 black pens, and 2 purple pens. A customer reaches into the jar and chooses a pen at random. Find the probability that the customer chooses a pen of the given color.

1. red   **2.** green   **3.** black   **4.** purple

A standard deck of 52 cards is shuffled and a card is drawn at random. Find the odds in favor of and against each of the following events.

5.   a 9 is drawn   **6.**   a 3 of diamonds is drawn

7.   a black king is drawn   **8.**   a red card is drawn

BENCHMARK 5
(Chapters 9, 10, and 11)

Find the number of ways you can arrange the given number of letters in the word.

9. THIS, 2 of the letters

10. BLACK, 3 of the letters

11. BIKE, 4 of the letters

12. MOTHERS, 5 of the letters

Students are being selected for various school awards. Find the number of possible combinations for each award given the number of each award and the number of students nominated.

13. 2 students from 5 nominated

14. 4 students from 6 nominated

15. 2 students from 11 nominated

16. 3 students from 7 nominated

You roll a number cube. Find the probability of each outcome.

17. a number less than 5 or an even number

18. an odd number or a prime number

A bag contains 7 blue, 4 red, and 5 green marbles. You randomly draw 2 marbles, one at a time. Find the probability:

19. of drawing a red marble, which you replace, and then drawing a blue marble

20. of drawing two green marbles without replacement

21. of drawing a red marble, which you do not replace, and then drawing a green marble

Benchmark 1

A. Expressions, Equations, and Inequalities

1. 30   **2.** 3   **3.** 2.7   **4.** $\frac{3}{2}$ **5.** 81   **6.** 4.41

7. 18   **8.** 26   **9.** 14   **10.** $\frac{y+4}{6}$ **11.** $2q^2 - 4$

12. $6w + 8$ **13.** $\frac{12}{q} \le 5$ **14.** $2h + 5 = 23$

15. $12 < w - 4 \le 20$

Quiz

1. 2   **2.** 4   **3.** 7   **4.** 66   **5.** 8   **6.** 6
7. $4(2y) + 8$ **8.** $6x^2 - 15$ **9.** $b + 12 = 2b$
10. $10 \le 3q \le 15$

B. Problem Solving

1. Yes   **2.** No   **3.** No   **4.** No   **5.** Yes   **6.** Yes
7. *You know:* The short trail is 2 km long and the long trail is 5 km long. You ride 3 laps on the short trail and *x* laps on the long. The total distance you ride is 21 km.   *You want to find out:* How many laps on the long trail do you need to ride a total of 21 km?   **8.** Number of laps on the short trail • Length of the short trail (km) + Number of laps on the long trail • Length of the long trail (km) = Total distance (km)   **9.** 3   **10.** 4   **11.** 2   **12.** 4
13. 4   **14.** 1

Quiz

1. No   **2.** Yes   **3.** Yes   **4.** Yes   **5.** Yes   **6.** No
7. *You know:* Jim's grandmother walks down the hall 90 yards, across 20 yards, up the hall 90 yards, and across 20 yards. She walks the length of the hall 9 times and she walks the width of the hall *x* times. She wants to walk a total of 970 yards. *You want to find out:* How many times does she need to walk the width of the hall to walk a total of 970 yards.
Verbal model:
Number of times she walks the length of the hall • Length of the hall (yd) + Number of times she walks the width of the hall • Width of the hall (yd) = Total distance (yd)   **8.** 4   **9.** 2   **10.** 1

C. Representations of Functions

1. Domain: 0, 1, 2, 3; Range: 1, 3, 5, 7
2. Domain: $-5, -10, -15, -20$; Range: 1, 2, 3, 4
3. Domain: $-6, -4, -1, 0$; Range: 0, 100, 400, 600   **4.** Yes   **5.** Yes   **6.** Yes   **7.** $y = \frac{x}{2}$

8. $y = x - 4$ **9.** $y = x + 9$ **10.** $y = -x$

11.

Input, x	3	6	9	12	15
Output, y	2	4	6	8	10

Range: 2, 4, 6, 8, 10

12.

Input, x	−5	−4	−3	−2	−1
Output, y	−6.1	−5.1	−4.1	−3.1	−2.1

Range: −6.1, −5.1, −4.1, −3.1, −2.1

13.

Input, x	1	2	4	7	9
Output, y	3	1	−3	−9	−13

Range: −13, −9, −3, 1, 3

14.

Input, x	20	30	40	50	60
Output, y	$\frac{21}{2}$	$\frac{31}{2}$	$\frac{41}{2}$	$\frac{51}{2}$	$\frac{61}{2}$

Range: $\frac{21}{2}, \frac{31}{2}, \frac{41}{2}, \frac{51}{2}, \frac{61}{2}$

15.

Input, x	2	5	6	8	9
Output, y	16	19	20	22	23

Range: 16, 19, 20, 22, 23

16.

Input, x	−3	−1	4	8	11
Output, y	15	5	−20	−40	−55

Range: −55, −40, −20, 5, 15

17.

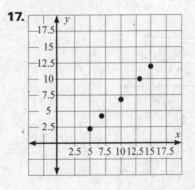

Answers continued

18.

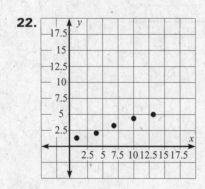

19.

20.

21.

22.

Quiz

1. Domain: 7, 10, 14, 17; Range: 23, 35, 51, 63

2. Domain: $-10, -8, -5, -4$; Range: 90, 54, 15, 6

3. Domain: $-3, -2, -1, 0$; Range: $-\frac{3}{8}, -\frac{1}{4}, -\frac{1}{8}, 0$

4. No   **5.** No   **6.** Yes   **7.** $y = 5x$ **8.** $y = -2x$

9. $y = x - 7$ **10.** $y = \frac{3}{2}x$

11.

Input, *x*	-3	-1	2	5	6
Output, *y*	22	14	2	-10	-14

Range: $-14, -10, 2, 14, 22$

12.

Input, *x*	10	12	14	16	18
Output, *y*	$\frac{13}{2}$	8	$\frac{19}{2}$	11	$\frac{25}{2}$

Range: $\frac{13}{2}, 8, \frac{19}{2}, 11, \frac{25}{2}$

13.

Input, *x*	1	9	13	19	23
Output, *y*	$\frac{5}{4}$	$\frac{21}{4}$	$\frac{29}{4}$	$\frac{41}{4}$	$\frac{49}{4}$

Range: $\frac{5}{4}, \frac{21}{4}, \frac{29}{4}, \frac{41}{4}, \frac{49}{4}$

14.

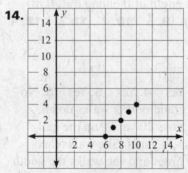

15.

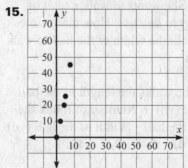

Answer Key

Answers continued

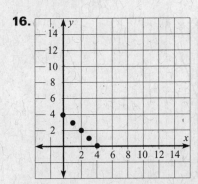

16.

D. Solving Equations in One Variable

1. $1.23, \dfrac{3}{2}, 1\dfrac{2}{3}, \sqrt{3}$ **2.** $-1.9, -\sqrt{0.04}, 0.08, \sqrt{2}$

3. $\sqrt{6}, 6.01, 6.1, 6\dfrac{1}{6}$ **4.** -1 **5.** 11 **6.** 4

7. 20 **8.** 8 **9.** -27 **10.** 2 **11.** -3 **12.** -24

13. $-\dfrac{10}{7}$ **14.** 9 **15.** -5 **16.** 3 **17.** -6

18. $\dfrac{2}{13}$ **19.** All real numbers   **20.** -20

21. No solution

Quiz

1. 5.3 **2.** 2.2 **3.** -15 **4.** $-\dfrac{6}{5}$ **5.** 10.5

6. 7 **7.** $\dfrac{2}{9}$ **8.** 110 **9.** 162 **10.** 6 **11.** 15

12. -20 **13.** -11 **14.** $\dfrac{2}{3}$ **15.** $\dfrac{5}{2}$

16. 0 **17.** All real numbers   **18.** -10

E. Proportion and Percent Problems

1. $\dfrac{2}{3}$ **2.** $\dfrac{1}{5}$ **3.** $\dfrac{1}{2}$ **4.** $\dfrac{12}{37}$ **5.** $\dfrac{2}{3}$ **6.** $\dfrac{27}{10}$ **7.** 14

8. 60 **9.** 10 **10.** 5 **11.** 6 **12.** 12 **13.** 57

14. 27 **15.** 180 **16.** 845 **17.** 15 **18.** 7

Quiz

1. $\dfrac{2}{5}$ **2.** $\dfrac{3}{4}$ **3.** $\dfrac{1}{14}$ **4.** $15\dfrac{1}{3}$ **5.** 30 **6.** 25

7. 52 **8.** 163 **9.** 9

F. Rewriting Equations in Two or More Variables

1. $P = \dfrac{I}{rt}$ **2.** $r = \sqrt{\dfrac{A}{\pi}}$ **3.** $V = E - F + 2$

4. $w = \dfrac{V}{\ell h}$ **5.** $h = \dfrac{3V}{\pi r^2}$ **6.** $b_1 = \dfrac{2A}{h} - b_2$

7. $V = \dfrac{m}{d}$; 64 cm³   **8.** $d = \dfrac{40}{\sqrt{s}}$; 4 miles

9. $h = \dfrac{v^2}{64} + 2r$; 46 ft   **10.** $y = 2x - 10$

11. $y = -\dfrac{4}{3}x - \dfrac{8}{3}$ **12.** $y = -\dfrac{1}{9}x - 3$

13. $y = \dfrac{8}{3}x + 16$ **14.** $y = -\dfrac{25}{2}x + 75$

15. $y = -\dfrac{1}{2}x - \dfrac{3}{2}$

Quiz

1. $\ell = \dfrac{P}{4}$ **2.** $h = \dfrac{V}{\pi r^2}$ **3.** $a = 2s - b - c$

4. $\ell = \dfrac{S}{\pi r} - r$ **5.** $v = 16t + \dfrac{h - c}{t}$

6. $w = \dfrac{S - 2\ell h}{2\ell + 2h}$ **7.** 3 ohms

8. $n = \dfrac{s}{180} + 2$; 15 sides   **9.** $c = \dfrac{1}{(1 - e)^2}$; 16

10. $y = \dfrac{1}{2}x - 2$ **11.** $y = -\dfrac{3}{7}x + 2$

12. $y = -7x + \dfrac{7}{3}$ **13.** $y = -\dfrac{4}{5}x - \dfrac{9}{5}$

14. $y = -\dfrac{8}{3}x - \dfrac{2}{3}$ **15.** $y = 6x + 9$

Benchmark 2

A. Graphing Linear Equations

1–6.

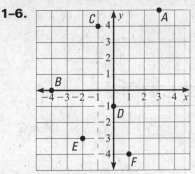

1. Quadrant I   **2.** x-axis   **3.** Quadrant II
4. y-axis   **5.** Quadrant III   **6.** Quadrant IV
7. Yes, it is a solution.   **8.** Yes, it is a solution.
9. No, it is not a solution.   **10.** No, it is not a
solution.   **11.** Yes, it is a solution.   **12.** No, it is
not a solution.

13.

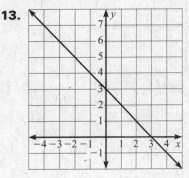

Answers continued

14.

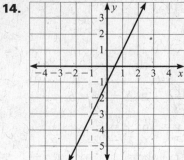

15.

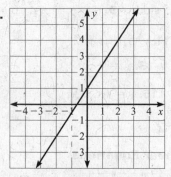

16.

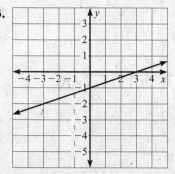

17.

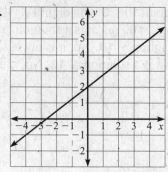

18.

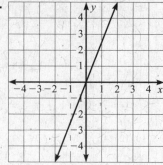

19.

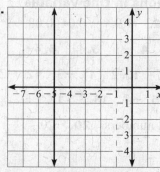

20.

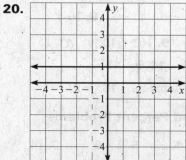

21.

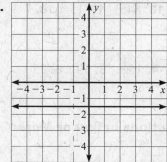

22.

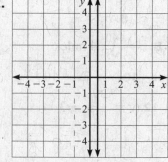

Answers continued

23.

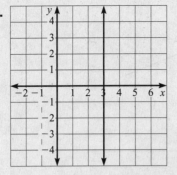

24.

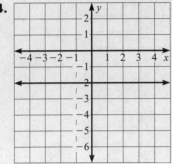

Quiz

1–6.

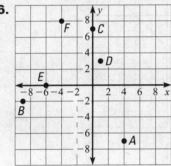

1. Quadrant IV   **2.** Quadrant III   **3.** *y*-axis
4. Quadrant I   **5.** *x*-axis   **6.** Quadrant II
7. Yes, it is a solution.   **8.** No, it is not a solution.
9. No, it is not a solution.   **10.** Yes, it is a
solution.   **11.** No, it is not a solution.
12. Yes, it is a solution.

13.

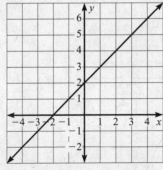

14.

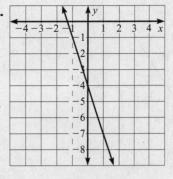

15.

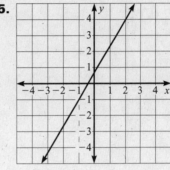

16.

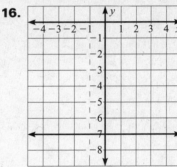

17.

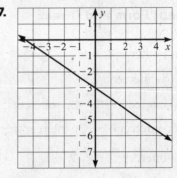

18.

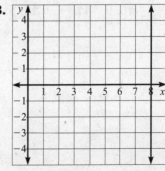

Answers *continued*

19.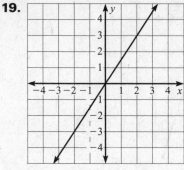

20.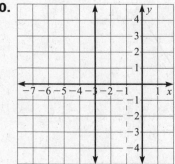

21.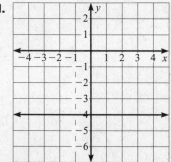

B. Slope-Intercept Form and Direct Variation

1. x-intercept: -6, y-intercept: -6

2. x-intercept: $-\frac{2}{3}$, y-intercept: $\frac{8}{3}$

3. x-intercept: 2, y-intercept: 18 **4.** x-intercept: 0, y-intercept: 0 **5.** x-intercept: $-\frac{1}{4}$, y-intercept: $\frac{3}{2}$

6. x-intercept: $\frac{1}{6}$, y-intercept: $-\frac{1}{2}$ **7.** -1

8. Undefined **9.** $-\frac{1}{8}$ **10.** 0 **11.** $-\frac{4}{3}$ **12.** 5

13.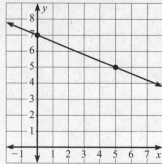

14.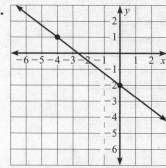

15.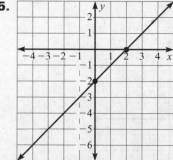

16.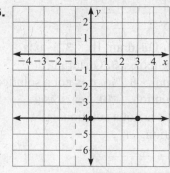

17.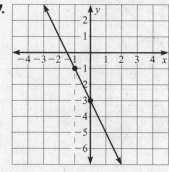

Answer Key

18.

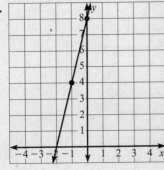

19. Yes; $-\dfrac{7}{8}$ **20.** No **21.** Yes; $\dfrac{5}{9}$ **22.** Yes; $-\dfrac{1}{47}$

23. Yes; -1 **24.** No **25.** $y = -\dfrac{1}{3}x; -4$

26. $y = 2x; 64$ **27.** $y = -\dfrac{1}{2}x; -9$

28. $y = \dfrac{2}{9}x; 6$ **29.** $y = -\dfrac{7}{5}x; -140$

30. $y = \dfrac{1}{2}x; 37$

Quiz

1. x-intercept: $-\dfrac{1}{4}$, y-intercept: $\dfrac{3}{2}$ **2.** x-intercept:

3, y-intercept: -1 **3.** x-intercept: 1.25,

y-intercept: 5 **4.** $-\dfrac{9}{11}$ **5.** 0 **6.** -1

7.

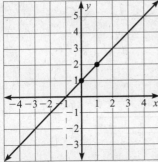

8.

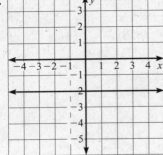

9.

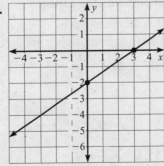

10. Yes; $-\dfrac{4}{5}$ **11.** No **12.** Yes; $\dfrac{7}{4}$

13. $y = -\dfrac{5}{2}x; -50$ **14.** $y = 3x; 129$

15. $y = -\dfrac{3}{2}x; -96$

C. Writing Linear Equations

1. $y = 6x - 4$ **2.** $y = -x + 3$ **3.** $y = \dfrac{3}{5}x - 5$

4. $y = \dfrac{2}{5}x - 3$ **5.** $y = -4x + 5$

6. $y = -\dfrac{1}{3}x - 2$ **7.** $y = \dfrac{4}{3}x + 6$

8. $y = -\dfrac{1}{4}x + \dfrac{11}{4}$ **9.** $y = -6x + 22$

10. $y = \dfrac{3}{2}x - \dfrac{21}{2}$ **11.** $y = -\dfrac{2}{3}x + 4$

12. $y = 2x - 2$ **13.** $y = \dfrac{2}{3}x - 3$

14. $y = -\dfrac{1}{4}x + 2$ **15.** $y = \dfrac{1}{2}x - \dfrac{5}{2}$

16. $y = \dfrac{3}{4}x + \dfrac{1}{4}$ **17.** $y = -x - 2$

18. $y = -\dfrac{1}{3}x + \dfrac{2}{3}$ **19.** $y + 1 = \dfrac{2}{3}(x - 3)$

20. $y - 0 = -\dfrac{1}{4}(x - 4)$ **21.** $y + 4 = \dfrac{1}{2}(x + 3)$

22. $y - 1 = \dfrac{3}{4}(x - 1)$ **23.** $y - 3 = -(x + 5)$

24. $y - 2 = -\dfrac{1}{3}(x + 4)$ **25.** $-4x + y = 3$

26. $3x + y = 2$ **27.** $-3x + 2y = 3$
28. $4x + 3y = -1$ **29.** $2x + y = -3$
30. $3x + 4y = 1$

Quiz

1. $y = 4x + 3$ **2.** $y = -2x + 1$ **3.** $y = \dfrac{5}{2}x - 4$

4. $y = -\dfrac{1}{3}x - 5$ **5.** $y = \dfrac{1}{5}x - \dfrac{17}{5}$

6. $y - 7 = -\dfrac{3}{4}(x + 2)$ **7.** $y - 5 = -4(x - 1)$

8. $y = -\dfrac{1}{2}x + 2; x + 2y = 4$ **9.** $y = -\dfrac{4}{3}x - 3;$

$4x + 3y = -9$

D. Parallel and Perpendicular Lines

1. a and c are parallel.   **2.** d and e are perpendicular.   **3.** h and j are parallel. g is perpendicular to h and j.   **4.** $y = \frac{4}{3}x + 3$

5. $y = -\frac{1}{4}x + 3$ **6.** $y = -6x + 15$

7. $y = \frac{3}{2}x - 3$ **8.** $y = -\frac{2}{3}x$ **9.** $y = 2x + 8$

10. $y = -\frac{2}{3}x - 4$ **11.** $y = \frac{4}{3}x + 9$

12. $y = \frac{1}{8}x + \frac{19}{4}$ **13.** $y = -3x + 12$

14. $y = \frac{3}{2}x$ **15.** $y = -\frac{1}{2}x - 6$

Quiz

1. a and b are parallel. c is perpendicular to a and b.   **2.** d and e are perpendicular.

3. h and j are parallel.   **4.** $y = \frac{3}{8}x - 2$

5. $y = -\frac{2}{3}x + 1$ **6.** $y = 2x + 8$

7. $y = \frac{4}{3}x + 10$ **8.** $y = -\frac{1}{4}x - 2$

9. $y = -5x + 17$ **10.** $y = -3x + 10$

11. $y = \frac{3}{2}x - 5$ **12.** $y = -\frac{1}{2}x - 5$

13. $y = -\frac{2}{3}x - 2$ **14.** $y = \frac{4}{3}x - 5$ **15.** $y = \frac{1}{4}x$

E. Linear models

1. No correlation   **2.** Negative correlation
3. Positive correlation

4.

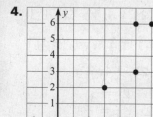

positive correlation

5.

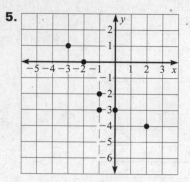

negative correlation

6. Answers may vary. Sample answer: $y = \frac{4}{5}x - 4$

7. Answers may vary. Sample answer: $y = \frac{5}{2}x - 4$

8.

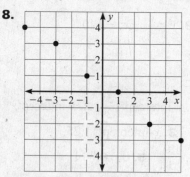

$y = -0.73x + 0.5; -2.4$

9.

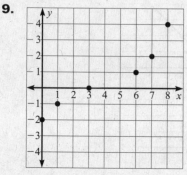

$y = 0.63x - 1.94; 0.58$

10.

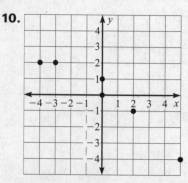

$y = -\frac{2}{3}x; -4\frac{2}{3}$

Answers continued

11.

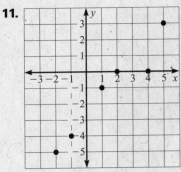

$y = x - 2.7;\ 1.3$

Quiz

1. No correlation   **2.** Positive correlation
3. Negative correlation

4a–c.

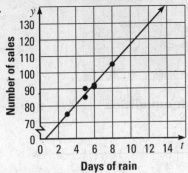

4b. Positive correlation   **4c.** $y = 6x + 57$
4d. $y = 5.85x + 57.5$ **4e.** 81 sales; 116 sales

Benchmark 3

A. Graphing Inequalities

1.

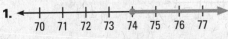

2.

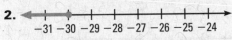

3.

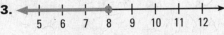

4.

5. $x > -2$ **6.** $x \le -10$ **7.** $x \ge 6$ **8.** $x < -5$
9. $-3 < x < 0$

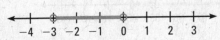

10. $x \le 2$ or $x \ge 9$

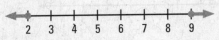

11. $-1 \le x < 6$

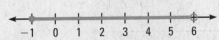

12. $x < 55$ or $x \ge 60$

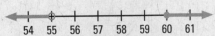

13.

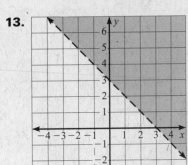

14.

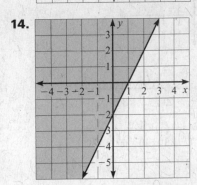

15.

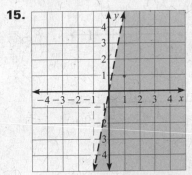

16.

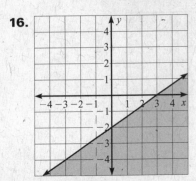

Answer Key

Answers continued

17.
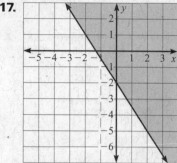

18.
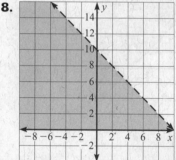

Quiz

1.
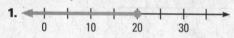

2.
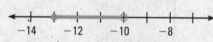

3. $x < 4$ **4.** $x \geq -5$

5. $-13 \leq x < -10$;
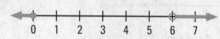

6. $x \leq 0$ or $x > 6$;
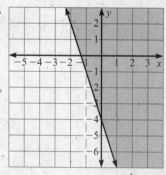

7.
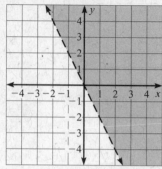

8.

9.
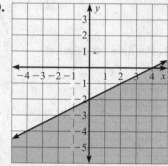

B. Solving Inequalities

1. $p > 3.3$
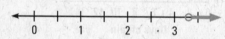

2. $m \leq 7$
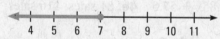

3. $k > -33$
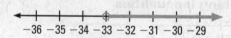

4. $t \geq -\dfrac{31}{5}$
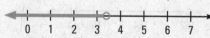

5. $r < 3.4$
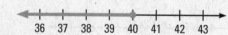

6. $m \leq 40$
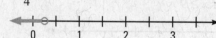

7. $x < \dfrac{1}{4}$

Answer Key

Answers continued

8. $d \geq 27$

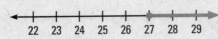

9. $c \geq -6$

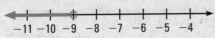

10. $z < -9$

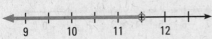

11. $w < 11.5$

12. $n \leq -40$

13. $x > 4$

14. $t \geq \dfrac{1}{2}$

15. $q > 20$

16. $v \leq 2$

17. $n \geq -2$

18. $a < -\dfrac{1}{2}$

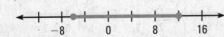

19. $3 < a < 5$

20. $-6 \leq x \leq 12$

21. $-6 \leq p \leq -3$

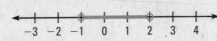

22. $-2 < n \leq -1$

23. $-9 < w < -3$

24. $-1 < j < 2$

25. $a \leq -6$ or $a > -3$

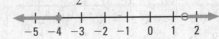

26. $n < -3$ or $n \geq 4$

27. $y < -5$ or $y > -1$

28. $k \leq -4$ or $k > \dfrac{3}{2}$

29. $b \leq 1$ or $b \geq 2$

30. All real numbers

Quiz

1. $y > -2.4$

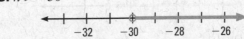

2. $b \leq 7$

3. $n > -30$

Answer Key

Answer Key

4. $k \geq -\frac{10}{3}$

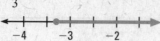

5. $d < -3.8$

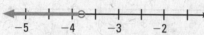

6. $a \leq 51$

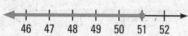

7. $x < 2$

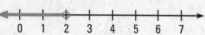

8. $x \geq 28$

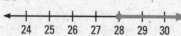

9. $c \geq -4$

10. $z < -24$

11. $y < 41.4$

12. $b \leq -480$

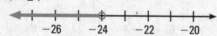

13. $x > 5$

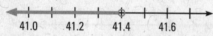

14. $s \geq \frac{2}{11}$

15. $p > \frac{1}{4}$

16. $r \leq 5$

17. $m \leq 1$

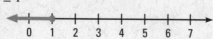

18. $z > 2$

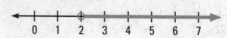

19. $3 < g < 6$

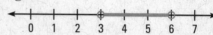

20. $-21 \leq x \leq 14$

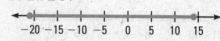

21. $-7 \leq a \leq -1$

22. $-1 < n \leq -\frac{1}{3}$

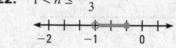

23. $-42 < t \leq -14$

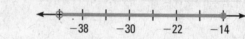

24. $-14 < j < -10$

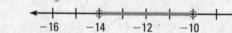

25. $x \leq 6$ or $x > 10$

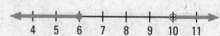

26. $x \leq -8$ or $x > -1$

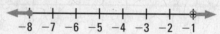

27. All real numbers

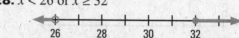

28. $x < 26$ or $x \geq 32$

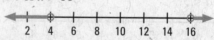

29. $x < 4$ or $x > 16$

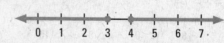

30. $x \leq 3$ or $x \geq 4$

Answers *continued*

C. Absolute Value Equations and Inequalilties

1. $x = 12$ or $x = -12$ **2.** $y = 2.4$ or $y = -2.4$

3. $b = \frac{2}{3}$ or $b = -\frac{2}{3}$ **4.** $m = 44$ or $m = -44$

5. $r = 6\frac{5}{8}$ or $r = -6\frac{5}{8}$ **6.** $p = 0.9$ or $p = -0.9$

7. $x = 0$ or $x = -6$ **8.** $c = 0$ or $c = 4$

9. $p = \frac{27}{4}$ or $p = -\frac{13}{4}$ **10.** $t = 4$ or $t = \frac{4}{3}$

11. $z = 1$ or $z = 4$ **12.** $a = \frac{5}{6}$ or $a = \frac{25}{6}$

13. $5 < x < 9$

14. $a \leq \frac{1}{2}$ or $a \geq \frac{7}{2}$

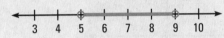

15. $n < -16$ or $n > 6$

16. $t \leq -\frac{1}{3}$ or $t \geq -\frac{2}{9}$

17. $-\frac{5}{2} < q < 2$

18. $0 \leq f \leq \frac{4}{5}$

Quiz

1. $a = 14$ or $a = -14$ **2.** $c = 9.7$ or $x = -9.7$

3. $x = \frac{4}{9}$ or $x = -\frac{4}{9}$ **4.** $n = 38$ or $n = -38$

5. $s = 1\frac{6}{7}$ or $s = -1\frac{6}{7}$ **6.** $q = 0.3$ or $q = -0.3$

7. $x = -1$ or $x = -7$ **8.** $u = -\frac{4}{3}$ or $u = \frac{8}{3}$

9. $q = \frac{43}{2}$ or $q = -\frac{37}{2}$ **10.** $t = -\frac{1}{2}$ or $t = -\frac{5}{4}$

11. $y = -\frac{3}{4}$ or $y = \frac{9}{4}$ **12.** $r = -65$ or $r = 95$

---

13. $-33 < x < 103$

14. $a \leq -\frac{3}{7}$ or $a \geq 1$

15. $t < -63$ or $t > 57$

16. $t \leq -0.85$ or $t \geq -0.65$

17. $-\frac{26}{3} < b < \frac{22}{3}$

18. $-1 \leq k \leq 2$

D. Solving Linear Systems by Graphing

1. yes   **2.** yes   **3.** no   **4.** no   **5.** no
6. yes   **7.** $(4, 3)$ **8.** $(3, 3)$ **9.** $(-2, 3)$
10. $(2, -1)$ **11.** $(-1, 3)$ **12.** $(3, -3)$
13. $(1, 4)$ **14.** $(2, 2)$ **15.** $(5, -2)$
16. no solution; the lines are parallel
17. infinitely many solutions; both equations represent the same line   **18.** no solution; the lines are parallel   **19.** no solution; the lines are parallel
20. infinitely many solutions; both equations represent the same line   **21.** infinitely many solutions; both equations represent the same line

Quiz

1. yes   **2.** no   **3.** yes   **4.** $(2, -1)$ **5.** $(-3, -2)$
6. $(4, 1)$ **7.** $(2, 0)$ **8.** no solution; the lines are parallel   **9.** $(-1, -1)$ **10.** $(5, 2)$ **11.** $(3, -5)$
12. infinitely many solutions; both equations represent the same line

E. Solving Linear Systems Using Algebra

1. $(1, 7)$ **2.** $(0, -3)$ **3.** $(-2, 1)$ **4.** $(-1, -2)$
5. $(2, 1)$ **6.** $(-1, 1)$ **7.** $(3, 2)$ **8.** $(-1, 4)$
9. $(2, -5)$ **10.** $(-6, -7)$ **11.** $(-1, -2)$

12. $(0, 3)$ **13.** $(-4, 2)$ **14.** $(2, 2)$ **15.** $(4, 3)$
16. $(2, -2)$ **17.** $(-4, -2)$ **18.** $(3, 6)$

Quiz

1. $(4, 2)$ **2.** $(1, 6)$ **3.** $(-3, -2)$ **4.** $(-3, -2)$

5. $(-1, 1)$ **6.** $(1, 2)$ **7.** $(3, 2)$ **8.** $(-1, -1)$
9. $(-2, 4)$ **10.** subtracting equations; $(1, 4)$
11. substitution; $(2, 4)$ **12.** multiplying first;
$(-2, 1)$ **13.** 5 times on the Ferris wheel and
7 times on the roller coaster

F. Solving Systems of Linear Inequalities

1.
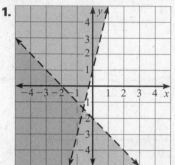

2.
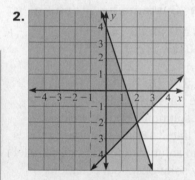

3.
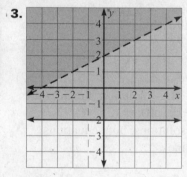

4.
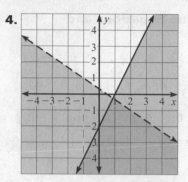

5.
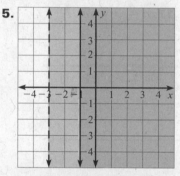

6.
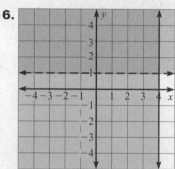

7.
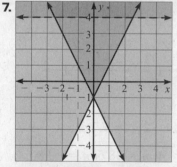

8.
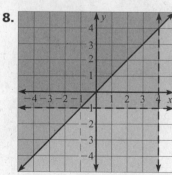

Answers continued

9.
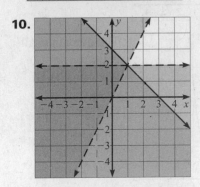

10.
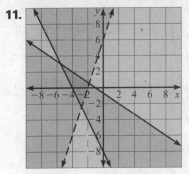

11.
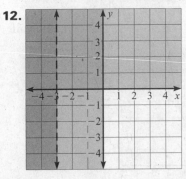

12.
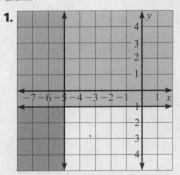

13. $y \leq -4x, y > -4x - 3$
14. $y < -3x + 3, y > 3x - 1$
15. $y > -2x - 1, y < 3, x \leq 4$

Quiz

1.
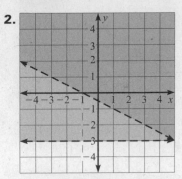

2.
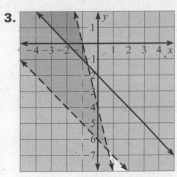

3.
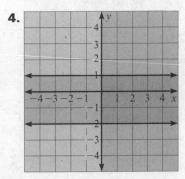

4.

5.

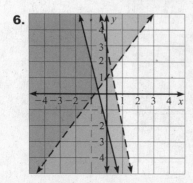

6.

7. $y > -2x - 5, y < -x - 1$

8. $y < 2, x > -2, x < -1$

9. $y \leq -3x + 6, y < -\frac{1}{2}x - 2, y < 3x - 6$

Benchmark 4

A. Properties of Exponents

1. 8^9 **2.** 5^{13} **3.** $(-6)^{12}$ **4.** d^{17} **5.** r^{20}

6. k^6 **7.** 10^{18} **8.** $(-6)^{16}$ **9.** t^{15}

10. b^{16} **11.** $(p + 5)^{14}$ **12.** $(h - 1)^{45}$

13. $5^6 \cdot 4^6$ **14.** $27g^3h^3$ **15.** $36c^2d^2$

16. $16p^4$ **17.** $-125t^3$ **18.** $-64a^2$

19. 18^6 **20.** 2^{32} **21.** $(-25)^2$ **22.** 4^{12}

23. n^4 **24.** w^2 **25.** $\dfrac{2^3}{5^3} = \dfrac{8}{125}$

26. $\dfrac{5^2}{8^2} = \dfrac{25}{64}$ **27.** $\dfrac{1}{p^8}$ **28.** $\dfrac{r^6}{s^6}$ **29.** $-\dfrac{u^9}{v^9}$

30. $-\dfrac{32}{b^5}$ **31.** $\dfrac{1}{11^2} = \dfrac{1}{121}$ **32.** 1

33. $\dfrac{1}{4^3} = 64$ **34.** $\dfrac{1}{(-3)^4} = \dfrac{1}{81}$

35. $6^2 = 36$ **36.** 1

Quiz

1. 7^{10} **2.** $(-8)^{13}$ **3.** y^{29} **4.** 6^{15} **5.** $(-4)^{21}$

6. s^{12} **7.** $(a + 11)^{32}$ **8.** $8^{13} \cdot 2^{13}$

9. $-(5)^7 j^7 k^7 = -78{,}125 j^7 k^7$ **10.** 3^{13}

11. v^9 **12.** $-\dfrac{3^3}{4^3} = -\dfrac{27}{64}$ **13.** $\dfrac{16}{h^2}$

14. $-\dfrac{p^{15}}{q^{15}}$ **15.** 1 **16.** $-\dfrac{1}{2^5} = -\dfrac{1}{32}$

17. $7^2 = 49$ **18.** 1

Algebra 1
Benchmark Answer Key

A16

B. Exponential Functions

1. 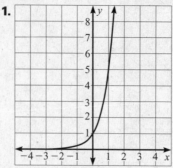 ; The domain is all real numbers. The range is all positive real numbers.

2. 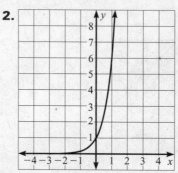 ; The domain is all real numbers. The range is all positive real numbers.

3. 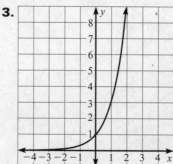 ; The domain is all real numbers. The range is all positive real numbers.

4. 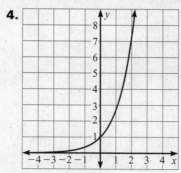 ; The domain is all real numbers. The range is all positive real numbers.

5. 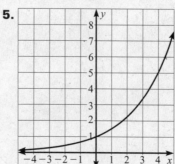 ; The domain is all real numbers. The range is all positive real numbers.

Answers *continued*

6. 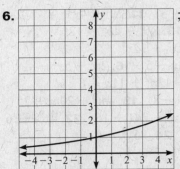 ; The domain is all real numbers. The range is all positive real numbers.

7a. $P = 245{,}000(1.018)^t$ **7b.** 292,849 people
8a. $h = 3.75(1.043)^t$ **8b.** 5.48 in.

9. 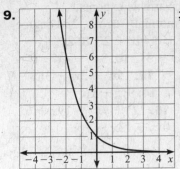 ; The domain is all real numbers. The range is all positive real numbers.

10. 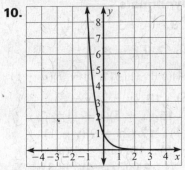 ; The domain is all real numbers. The range is all positive real numbers.

11. 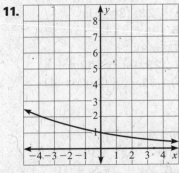 ; The domain is all real numbers. The range is all positive real numbers.

12. 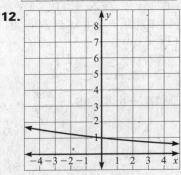 ; The domain is all real numbers. The range is all positive real numbers.

13. 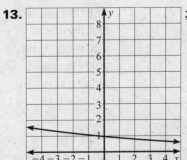 ; The domain is all real numbers. The range is all positive real numbers.

14. 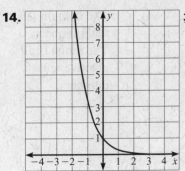 ; The domain is all real numbers. The range is all positive real numbers.

15a. $E = 95(0.75)^t$ **15b.** 23 essays
16a. $T = 475(0.92)^t$ **16b.** 136°

Quiz

1. 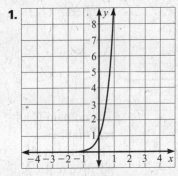 ; The domain is all real numbers. The range is all positive real numbers.

2. 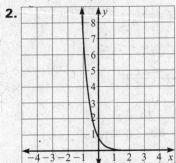 ; The domain is all real numbers. The range is all positive real numbers.

Answers *continued*

3. 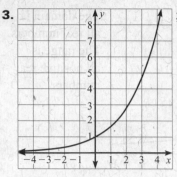 ; The domain is all real numbers. The range is all positive real numbers.

4. 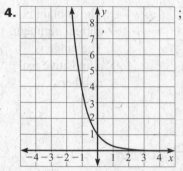 ; The domain is all real numbers. The range is all positive real numbers.

5. 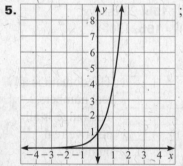 ; The domain is all real numbers. The range is all positive real numbers.

6. 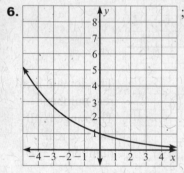 ; The domain is all real numbers. The range is all positive real numbers.

7a. $V = 5000(1.058)^t$ **7b.** \$63,216
8a. $W = 45(0.975)^t$ **8b.** 2 pounds

C. Adding, Subtracting, and Multiplying Polynomials

1. Yes; 1st degree monomial **2.** No; variable exponent **3.** Yes; 4th degree binomial
4. Yes; 5th degree trinomial **5.** No; negative exponent **6.** Yes; 3rd degree polynomial
7. $x^3 + 2x^2 - x + 2$ **8.** $-3x^2 - 5x + 5$
9. $3x^4 + 2x^3 - 4x^2 + 2x + 2$

10. $4x^3 + 3x^2 - x + 3$ **11.** $2x^2 + 4x - 8$
12. $5x^2 + x - 3$ **13.** $8b^5 + 4b^4 - 12b^3$
14. $4x^7 - 10x^6 - 2x^5 + 12x^4$
15. $2y^3 - 7y^2 + 13y - 5$ **16.** $2z^3 + 5z^2 - 14z + 3$ **17.** $2a^3 - 13a^2 + 11a + 6$
18. $6x^3 - 5x^2 + 6x + 8$ **19.** $4m^2 + 20m + 25$
20. $z^2 - 49$ **21.** $9x^2 - 24x + 16$ **22.** $4x^2 - 16$
23. $4s^2 + 4st + t^2$ **24.** $25x^2 - 4$

Quiz

1. Not a polynomial; negative exponent
2. Yes; 1st degree binomial **3.** Yes; 3rd degree polynomial **4.** No; variable exponent
5. Yes; 5th degree trinomial **6.** Yes; 2nd degree trinomial **7.** $2x^3 + x^2 + 4x + 2$ **8.** $2x^2 + 6x - 3$ **9.** $4x^2 + 2x - 3$ **10.** $3x^2 - 4x - 6$
11. $6z^5 - 12z^3 + 15z^2$ **12.** $15x^3 - 2x^2 - 36x - 7$
13. $4b^6 - 8b^5 - 4b^3$ **14.** $9y^2 - 16$
15. $k^2 - 18k + 81$ **16.** $2x^3 + 7x^2 - 19x + 6$
17. $4p^2 - 9r^2$ **18.** $10x^2 - 13x - 3$
19. $9y^2 + 30y + 25$

D. Factoring Polynomials

1. $-6, 2$ **2.** $1, 8$ **3.** $-4, -3$ **4.** $0, 4$
5. $-7, 0$ **6.** $-\frac{3}{4}, 0$ **7.** $0, \frac{7}{5}$ **8.** $0, \frac{1}{2}$
9. $0, \frac{1}{5}$ **10.** $(z + 4)(z + 3)$ **11.** $(n - 7)(n - 1)$
12. $(m + 4)(m - 6)$ **13.** $(y - 2)(y - 3)$
14. $(t - 3)(t + 5)$ **15.** $(x + 5)(x + 1)$
16. $(2x - 5)(2x + 1)$ **17.** $(2y - 9)(y - 1)$
18. $-(2z + 3)(2z - 5)$ **19.** $(3m - 4)(m - 2)$
20. $-(2x - 3)(x - 7)$ **21.** $(3t - 4)(t + 3)$
22. $(3x + 1)(3x - 1)$ **23.** $(2s + 1)^2$
24. $(2m - 3n)^2$ **25.** $(4t + 3)(4t - 3)$
26. $(5z - 2)^2$ **27.** $(x + 4y)^2$
28. $(2t + 3)(t^2 - 5)$ **29.** $(m - 5)(2m + n)$
30. $(3x^2 + 1)(x - 7)$ **31.** $(x + 2y)(x - 4)$

Quiz

1. $4y(y^2 - 5)$ **2.** $5m^2(2m^2 + 3)$
3. $(t - 9)(t + 2)$ **4.** $(x - 3)(x + 9)$
5. $(s - 7)(4s + 1)$ **6.** $(5y + 2)(2y + 1)$
7. $(4x^2 + y)(4x^2 - y)$ **8.** $(5s + 2t)(5s - 2t)$
9. $(m - 3n)^2$ **10.** $(2x + 6y)^2$
11. $(x - 3)(x + 4y)$ **12.** $(t - 2)(t + 3s)$
13. $-3, 0$ **14.** $-5, 4$ **15.** $-2, 8$
16. $-5, \frac{1}{3}$ **17.** $\frac{1}{2}, \frac{3}{2}$ **18.** $-8, 8$ **19.** $-\frac{2}{3}, \frac{2}{3}$
20. $-\frac{5}{3}$ **21.** $\frac{1}{2}$

Benchmark 5

A. Graphing Quadratic Functions

1.

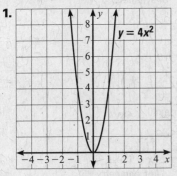

Same vertex, $(0, 0)$, and axis of symmetry, $x = 0$. The graph is narrower than the graph of $y = x^2$ — it is a vertical stretch (by a factor of 4) of the graph of $y = x^2$.

2.

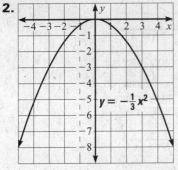

Same vertex, $(0, 0)$, and axis of symmetry, $x = 0$. The graph is wider than the graph of $y = x^2$ — it is a vertical shrink (by a factor of $\frac{1}{3}$) with a reflection in the x-axis of the graph of $y = x^2$.

3.

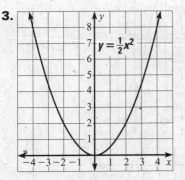

Same vertex, $(0, 0)$, and axis of symmetry, $x = 0$. The graph is wider than the graph of $y = x^2$ — it is a vertical shrink (by a factor of $\frac{1}{2}$) of the graph of $y = x^2$.

4.

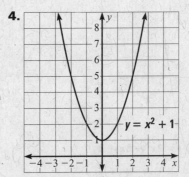

Graph also opens up, has the same axis of symmetry, $x = 0$. The vertex $(0, 1)$, is different. The graph of $y = x^2 + 1$ is a vertical translation (of 1 unit up) of the graph of $y = x^2$.

5.

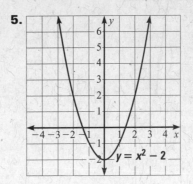

Graph also opens up, has the same axis of symmetry, $x = 0$. The vertex $(0, -2)$, is different. The graph of $y = x^2 - 2$ is a vertical translation (of 2 units down) of the graph of $y = x^2$.

6.

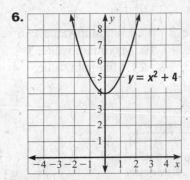

Graph also opens up, has the same axis of symmetry, $x = 0$. The vertex $(0, 4)$, is different. The graph of $y = x^2 + 4$ is a vertical translation (of 4 units up) of the graph of $y = x^2$.

7. $x = -1$, $(-1, 8)$ **8.** $x = 4$, $(4, -9)$
9. $x = 2$, $(2, 4)$ **10.** $x = -2$, $(-2, -3)$
11. $x = 3$, $(3, 3)$ **12.** $x = \frac{3}{2}$, $\left(\frac{3}{2}, \frac{19}{2}\right)$

13.

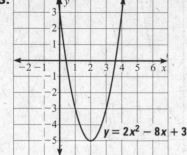

$y = 2x^2 - 8x + 3$

14.

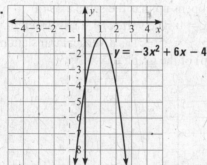

$y = -3x^2 + 6x - 4$

15.

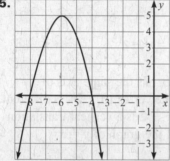

16. Maximum value, 3   **17.** Minimum value, −6
18. Minimum value, 4   **19.** Maximum value, 5
20. Maximum value, −2   **21.** Minimum value, −4

Quiz

1.

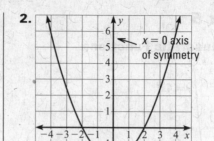

vertex (0, 0)
$x = 0$ axis of symmetry

2.

$x = 0$ axis of symmetry

vertex (0, −2)

3.

$x = 1$ axis of symmetry

vertex (1, 3)

4.

$x = 2$ axis of symmetry

vertex (2, −4)

5.

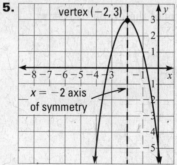

vertex (−2, 3)

$x = -2$ axis of symmetry

6.

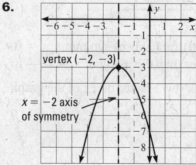

vertex (−2, −3)

$x = -2$ axis of symmetry

7. Minimum value, 7   **8.** Maximum value, -6

9. Minimum value, $-\frac{1}{8}$ **10.** Minimum value, -7

11. Maximum value, $5\frac{1}{2}$ **12.** Maximum value, 7

B. Solving Quadratic Equations

1. $-2, 1$ **2.** No solution   **3.** -2 **4.** 3
5. No solution   **6.** $-3, 2$ **7.** 0   **8.** ± 3
9. No solution   **10.** No solution   **11.** 0
12. ± 4 **13.** $-6, 2$ **14.** $-3, 1$ **15.** $-5, 7$
16. $-8, -4$ **17.** $-3, 9$ **18.** $-13, -3$
19. $-5.32, 1.32$ **20.** $-1, 1.67$ **21.** $-1.78, 0.28$
22. Factoring; $2x^2 - x - 6$ can be factored
easily   **23.** Factoring; $x^2 - 6x$ can be factored
easily   **24.** Quadratic formula; $4x^2 + 2x - 9$
cannot be factored   **25.** Square roots; write in the
form $x^2 = d$ **26.** Quadratic formula;
$x^2 - 3x - 6$ cannot be factored
27. Completing the square; $a = 1$ and b is even
28. $(2, 0)$ and $(-2, -4)$ **29.** $(3, 0)$ and $(1, -2)$
30. $(0, 2)$ and $(3, -4)$

Quiz

1. 4   **2.** No solution   **3.** $-3, 4$ **4.** ± 2
5. No solution   **6.** 0   **7.** $-2, 10$ **8.** $-13, 1$
9. $2, 12$ **10.** $0.23, 1.43$ **11.** $-2.16, 1.16$
12. $-1.83, 3.83$ **13.** $(0, -4)$ and $(-1, -5)$
14. $(-2, 8)$ and $(1, -4)$ **15.** $(-1, 3)$

C. Comparing Linear, Exponential, and Quadratic Models

1. Linear function   **2.** Exponential function
3. Quadratic function   **4.** Exponential   **5.** Linear
6. Quadratic   **7.** Linear   **8.** Linear function
9. Quadratic function   **10.** Exponential function
11. Quadratic function; $y = 0.2x^2$ **12.** Linear
function; $y = 3x - 2$ **13.** Linear function;
$y = 2x + 3$ **14.** Quadratic function; $y = 3x^2$

Quiz

1. Quadratic function   **2.** Linear function
3. Exponential function   **4a.** Logarithmic
b. The cost of materials for 0 units. **5.** Linear
function   **6.** Exponential function   **7.** Quadratic
function   **8.** Linear function; $y = 2x - 1$
9. Quadratic function; $y = 4x^2$ **10.** Quadratic
function; $y = 0.1x^2$ **11.** Linear function;
$y = 4x + 2$

D. Analyzing Data

1. All students of a school, stratified random sample
2. Voters in the county, self-selected sample (those
who volunteer to return the survey)
3. Members of the organization, random sample
4. Yes. Answers will vary. Sample answer: Students
who do not participate in school sports will hold
significantly different opinions.   **5.** Yes. Answers
will vary. Sample answer: The question suggests
that participation is school sports is important for
fitness. An unbiased question: "What factors are
important for staying fit?"   **6.** 10 in.   **7.** 41.5 in.
8. 36 in.   **9.** Answers will vary. Sample answer:
The median best represents the data. The mode
and the mean are significantly less than most of the
data.   **10.** Range of $A = 3.2$, range of $B = 1.6$;
The data in A cover a wider interval.   **11.** Mean
absolute deviation of $A = 0.832$, mean absolute
deviation of $B = 0.42$; The average variation from
the mean is greater for the data in A.

12.

Player Scores

Stem	Leaves
7	4 8
5	0 2
6	1 4 4 6 7
7	1 2 5 5 6 9
8	0 2 3 4 5

key: 10 | 1 = 101 shots

13. Answers will vary. Sample answer: The scores
are clustered in the 90's, 100's, and 110's. There
are significantly more leaves for those three stems
than the other two stems.

14.

15.

Answer Key

Answers *continued*

16. Show 3   **17.** Pit tickets had the least number of tickets sold in Shows 1 and 3.   **18.** 204

Quiz

1. Concert attendees, convenience sample
2. Company employees, systematic sample
3. Yes. Answers will vary. Sample answer: People who do not go to action movies will hold significantly different opinions.   **4.** Yes. Answers will vary. Sample answer: The question suggests that violence in movies is not harmful. An unbiased question: "Is violence in movies harmful?"
5. 11 in.   **6.** 18.5 in.   **7.** 20.875 in.   **8.** Answers will vary. Sample answer: Both the mean and median represent the data. The mode is significantly less than most of the data.   **9.** Range of $A = 12$, range of $B = 10$; The data in A cover a wider interval.   **10.** Mean absolute deviation of $A = 3.04$, mean absolute deviation of $B = 3.2$; The average variation from the mean is greater for the data in B.

11.

Scores

Stem		Leaves				
0	3	3	7	7		
1	0	0	3	4	7	9
2	0	1	1	4	6	7
3	1	4	5			
4	1					

key: 3 | 1 = 31 points

12. Answers will vary. Sample answer: The scores are clustered in the 10's and 0's. There are significantly more leaves for those two stems than the other three stems.

13.

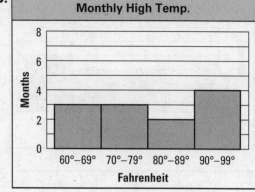

14.

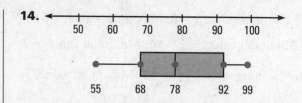

15. Jamal   **16.** Yes; Jamal won games 1 and 3.
17. 45

E. Probabilities of Simple and Compound Events

1. $\frac{3}{20}$ **2.** $\frac{3}{10}$ **3.** $\frac{7}{20}$ **4.** $\frac{1}{5}$ **5.** $1 : 25, 25 : 1$
6. $1 : 12, 12 : 1$ **7.** $1 : 3, 3 : 1$ **8.** $3 : 10,$ $10 : 3$ **9.** 6   **10.** 360   **11.** 24   **12.** 5040
13. 15   **14.** 56   **15.** 5   **16.** 210   **17.** $\frac{2}{3}$
18. $\frac{2}{3}$ **19.** $\frac{5}{6}$ **20.** $\frac{1}{12}$ **21.** $\frac{5}{33}$ **22.** $\frac{5}{44}$

Quiz

1. $\frac{1}{5}$ **2.** $\frac{2}{15}$ **3.** $\frac{1}{3}$ **4.** $\frac{1}{15}$ **5.** $1 : 12, 12 : 1$
6. $1 : 51, 51 : 1$ **7.** $1 : 25, 25 : 1$ **8.** $9 : 4,$ $4 : 9$ **9.** 12   **10.** 60   **11.** 24   **12.** 2520
13. 10   **14.** 15   **15.** 55   **16.** 35   **17.** $\frac{5}{6}$ **18.** $\frac{2}{3}$
19. $\frac{7}{64}$ **20.** $\frac{1}{12}$ **21.** $\frac{1}{12}$

Answer Key